The Doctrines and Discipline of the Free Methodist Church

Adopted August 23, 1860

Published By
Rev. B.T. Roberts
For the Free Methodist Church

First Fruits Press
Wilmore, Kentucky
c2016

The doctrines and discipline of the Free Methodist Church, adopted August 23, 1860.
Free Methodist Church of North America.

First Fruits Press, ©2016
Previously published by B.T. Roberts for the Free Methodist Church, 1860.

ISBN: 9781621715924 (print), 9781621715931 (digital), 9781621715948 (kindle)

Digital version at http://place.asburyseminary.edu/freemethodistbooks/18/

For all other uses, contact:

First Fruits Press
B.L. Fisher Library
Asbury Theological Seminary
204 N. Lexington Ave.
Wilmore, KY 40390
http://place.asburyseminary.edu/firstfruits

Free Methodist Church of North America.
 The doctrines and discipline of the Free Methodist Church, adopted August 23, 1860. -- [First edition] -- Wilmore, Kentucky : First Fruits Press, ©2016.
  125 pages ; 21 cm.
  Reprint. Previously published: Buffalo: B.T. Roberts for the Free Methodist Church, 1860.
  ISBN - 13: 9781621715924 (pbk.)
  1. Free Methodist Church of North America--Doctrines. 2. Free Methodist Church of North America--Discipline. I. Title.
BX8418 .A3 1860a   287.9

Cover design by Jon Ramsay

asburyseminary.edu
800.2ASBURY
204 North Lexington Avenue
Wilmore, Kentucky 40390

First Fruits
THE ACADEMIC OPEN PRESS OF ASBURY SEMINARY

First Fruits Press
The Academic Open Press of Asbury Theological Seminary
204 N. Lexington Ave., Wilmore, KY 40390
859-858-2236
first.fruits@asburyseminary.edu
asbury.to/firstfruits

THE DOCTRINES

AND

DISCIPLINE

OF THE

𝕱𝖗𝖊𝖊 𝕸𝖊𝖙𝖍𝖔𝖉𝖎𝖘𝖙 𝕮𝖍𝖚𝖗𝖈𝖍

ADOPTED AUGUST 23, 1860.

———•◆•———

BUFFALO:

PUBLISHED BY B. T. ROBERTS,

For the Free Methodist Church.

1860.

CLAPP, MATTHEWS & CO'S STEAM PRINTING HOUSE,
Office of the Buffalo Morning Express.

FREE METHODIST CHURCH.

THE Free Methodist Church had its origin in necessity and not in choice. It did not grow out of a secession, nor out of an unsuccessful attempt to bring about a reform in the government of the Church. Those concerned in its formation never expected a separation from the Methodist Episcopal Church, until they were unjustly excluded from its pale. They sought redress at the proper tribunal. It was not granted. Even a candid hearing was denied them. Thus thrown out, and the possibility of a restoration being cut off, and believing that God still called them to labor for the salvation of souls, they had no alternative but to form a new organization. In doctrine, discipline, and spirit they were Methodists, and hence they could not offer themselves to any other denomination.

The issue on which they were thrust out was between dead formalism, and the life and power of godliness, and so they could not feel at home with those branches of the Methodist family into whose formation other questions mainly entered.

Jesus has always had a people—a plain, humble, earnest people—to preach the Gospel to the poor, and to spread scriptural holiness throughout the world. We believe the Methodists were raised up for this purpose. God was with them, and gave them great success in saving souls.

But as they grew strong and wealthy, pride, and a love of popularity crept in among them. The Discipline was too generally unheeded. It became obvious to the most casual observer, that there was, among many of the ministers and members of the Methodist Episcopal Church in the United States, a very wide and **growing departure** from the original spirit of Methodism. This departure is also seen in the alterations that have been recently made in the Discipline.

In 1852 the rule requiring our houses of worship to be built "*plain and with free seats*," was effectually neutralized by adding the words, " wherever practicable." Conformity to the world was greatly encouraged in 1856 by repealing *the law* which had stood in the Discipline from the first, forbidding the reception of members until they had laid off " superfluous ornaments," and substituting a simple exhortation to " conform to the spirit of the apostolic precept," as though plain commands of God could be violated without violating their spirit.

In the Genesee Conference this departure from the old paths was hastened by the connection of several of its prominent members with secret societies. These, bound together by a tie unknown to the rest of the body, and laying their plans in the strictest secrecy, formed a solid nucleus, around which the formal and the aspiring naturally rallied. A portion of the Conference wished to adhere to primitive Methodism. They loved the doctrine of holiness, and preached it with success. Their labors were prospered, and their services were sought for. While they had the countenance of the bishops they were unmolested.

At the General Conference of the M. E. Church, held in 1856, the bishops took a decided stand against the enactment of a law excluding slave-holders from the church. The secret-society worldly-policy members of the Genesee Conference, some of whom had been radical abolitionists, sided with the bishops, on the slavery question. At its next session, thirty of them combined together not to take work unless Rev. L. Stiles, and Rev. I. C. Kingsley—men whose sympathies and labors were for the promotion of spiritual religion— were removed from the cabinet. They were transferred, and their places supplied by such men as the thirty (who with their adherents were henceforth known as " The Regency,") could render subservient to their purposes.

But the work of holiness went on. Dead and formal ministers were in no better demand than before. At the next session of the Genesee Conference, in a secret meeting held by the regency, they voted to bring Rev. B. T. Roberts, and Rev. W. C. Kendall to trial. Charges were preferred. Mr. Roberts was voted guilty of "immoral and unchristain conduct" for publishing in the *Northern Independent*, in an article entitled " New School Methodism," things that were not in that article, or in any other that he ever wrote.

His character was then passed, and he was sent out to preach. For the want of time Mr. Kendall's trial was deferred. At the next Conference, held in Perry, in October, 1858, secret meetings of the regency were held, as had been done at the two preceding sessions. Mr. Roberts was charged with " contumacy," for publishing and circulating a second edition of " New School Methodism," and a pamphlet signed by " Geo. W. Estes," which gave a short account of the trial of the year preceding. On this charge, and on the testimony of only one witness, whose veracity was fully impeached, Mr. Roberts was expelled from the Conference, and from the M. E. Church. Mr. McCreery was also expelled at the same time on the same charges.

Called of God to preach, they could not cease because the human authority with which they had been invested was thus taken away. The members of the church who had witnessed their labors and their spirit, thought they should still endeavor to save their fellow men. One hundred and ninety-five prominent laymen met in convention at Albion, Dec. 1st, 1858, and passed resolutions, expressing their entire and unabated confidence in the expelled preachers, and recommending them to continue to labor for the salvation of souls.

At the next session of the Genesee Conference, held at Brockport, in Oct. 1858, Reverends L. Stiles, C. D. Burlingham, J. A. Wells, and W. Cooley, were expelled for "contumacy," in sympathizing with those who had been expelled the year preceding. Reverends J. W. Reddy, and H. H. Farnsworth were located for the same cause.

Members of the Church who manifested an active sympathy with the expelled preachers, were themselves expelled in large numbers. Many were, without their consent, and contrary to their wishes, read out by the preachers as "withdrawn." Among both these classes were many of undoubted piety, and of long standing in the church, who had contributed largely by their money and their influence to its prosperity, and whose love for it was unabated.

Fifteen hundred members of the M. E. Church, within the bounds of the Genesee Conference, respectfully petitioned the General Conference, at its session in Buffalo, in May, 1860, to investigate the judicial action of the Genesee Conference. A committee of forty-two was appointed for this purpose. A me-

morial setting forth the grievances com-
plained of, and affidavits and documents
substantiating the complaints, were presented. A determined effort to get the
committee discharged was made by the
partisans of the majority of Genesee
Conference. *The committee was discharged,* and *investigation was suppressed.*

The appeal cases were summarily dis-
posed of. That of the Rev. C. D. Burlingham, who, from the time of his expulsion, desisted from all public efforts
to do good to the souls of men, was, without the shadow of a reason, sent back
for a new trial. Upon the first appeal
of Mr. Roberts—that from the verdict
of reproof—the committee stood equal-
ly divided. The other appeals were not
entertained, though the constitution of
the M. E. Church declares, in the most
emphatic manner, that the General Conference shall *not deprive* the ministers *of
the privilege of appeal.*

The same General Conference authorized the preachers to go beyond the
bounds of their charge to obtain a committee to try their members.

Under this new rule the work of expulsion went on. Pious men, long known for their strong attachment to Methodism, who were too conscientious and God-fearing, to give their sanction to what they believed to be great iniquities, were excommunicated.

Committees, imported from a distance for the purpose, expelled, after the mockery of a trial, devoted men of God. All hope of a change for the better being cut off, and it being evident that the authorities of the Methodist Episcopal Church were determined to put down what devout souls believed to be the work of God, a convention of laymen and ministers met at Pekin, Niagara Co., N. Y., on the 23d of August, 1860, and adopted the following form of Discipline.

We do no wish any to subscribe to it unless they believe it will be for the glory of God and the good of their souls. We have no desire to get up simply a large church; but we do hope that our societies will be composed, *exclusively*, of those who are *in earnest to gain heav-*

en, and who *are determined, by the grace of God*, to live up to the requirements of the Bible.

Where societies already organized design to unite with the Free Methodist Church, we recommend that they adopt the Discipline as a whole; and then, that each member be admitted in his individual capacity, as provided for in section third of chapter first, entitled " Of receiving members into the Church."

It is of the greatest importance that those who come into the new organization be of one heart and one mind.

CONTENTS.

CHAPTER I.

CHAPTER II.

CHAPTER III.

CHAPTER IV.

CHAPTER V.

CHAPTER VI.

CHAPTER VII.

CHAPTER VIII.

CHAPTER IX.

CHAPTER X.

CHAPTER XI.

CHAPTER XII.

CHAPTER XIII.

THE DOCTRINES AND DISCIPLINE

OF THE

FREE METHODIST CHURCH

CHAPTER I.

SECTION I.

ARTICLES OF RELIGION.

I. *Of Faith in the Holy Trinity.*

THERE is but one living and true God, everlasting, without body or parts, of infinite power, wisdom, and goodness; the maker and preserver of all things, visible and invisible. And in unity of this Godhead, there are three persons, of one substance, power, and eternity;—the Father, the Son, and the Holy Ghost.

II. *Of the Word, or Son of God, who was made very Man.*

The Son, who is the Word of the Father, the very and eternal God, of one substance with the Father, took man's nature in the womb of the blessed virgin; so that two whole and perfect natures, that is to say, the Godhead and manhood, were joined together in one person,

1

never to be divided, whereof is one Christ, very God and very man, who truly suffered, was crucified, dead and buried, to reconcile his Father to us, and to be a sacrifice, not only for original guilt, but also for actual sins of men.

III. *Of the Resurrection of Christ.*

Christ did truly rise again from the dead, and took again his body, with all things appertaining to the perfection of man's nature, wherewith he ascended into heaven, and there sitteth until he return to judge all men at the last day.

IV. *Of the Holy Ghost.*

The Holy Ghost, proceeding from the Father and the Son, is of one substance, majesty and glory, with the Father and the Son, very and eternal God.

V. *The Sufficiency of the Holy Scriptures for Salvation.*

The Holy Scriptures contain all things necessary to salvation: so that whatsoever is not read therein, nor may be proved thereby, is not to be required of any man, that it should be believed as an article of faith, or be thought requisite or necessary to salvation. In the name of the Holy Scripture, we do understand those canonical books of the Old and New Testament, of whose authority was never any doubt in the Church.

The Names of the Canonical Books.

Genesis,
Exodus,
Leviticus,
Numbers,
Deuteronomy,
Joshua,
Judges,
Ruth,
The First Book of Samuel,
The Second Book of Samuel,
The First Book of Kings,
The Second Book of Kings,
The First Book of Chronicles,
The Second Book of Chronicles,
The Book of Ezra,
The Book of Nehemiah,
The Book of Esther,
The Book of Job,
The Psalms,
The Proverbs,
Ecclesiastes, or the Preacher,
Cantica, or Songs of Solomon,
Four Prophets the greater,
Twelve Prophets the less:

All the books of the New Testament, as they are commonly received, we do receive and account canonical.

VI. *Of the Old Testament.*

The Old Testament is not contrary to the New; for both in the Old and New Testaments everlasting life is offered to mankind by Christ, who is the only Mediator between God and man. Wherefore they are not to be heard who feign that the old fathers did look only for transitory promises. Although the law given from God by Moses, as touching ceremonies and rites, doth not bind Christians, nor ought the civil precepts thereof of necessity to be received in any commonwealth; yet, notwithstanding, no Christian whatsoever is free from the obedience of the commandments which are called moral.

VII. *Of Original or Birth Sin.*

Original sin standeth not in the following of Adam, (as the Pelagians do vainly talk,) but it is the corruption of the nature of every man that naturally is engendered of the offspring of Adam, whereby man is very far gone from original righteousness, and of his own nature inclined to evil, and that continually.

VIII. *Of Free Will.*

The condition of man after the fall of Adam is such, that he cannot turn and prepare himself, by his own natural strength and works, to faith and calling upon God; wherefore we have no power to do good works, pleasant and acceptable to God, without the grace of God by Christ preventing us, that we may have a good will and working with us, when we have that good will.

IX.   *Of the Justification of Man.*

We are accounted righteous before God, only for the merit of our Lord and Saviour Jesus Christ by faith, and not for our own works or deservings: Wherefore, that we are justified by faith only, is a most wholesome doctrine, and very full of comfort.

X.   *Of Good Works.*

Although good works, which are the fruits of faith, and follow after justification, cannot put away our sins, and endure the severity of God's judgments; yet they are pleasing and acceptable to God in Christ, and spring out of a true and lively faith, insomuch that by them a lively faith may be as evidently known as a tree is discerned by its fruits.

XI.   *Of Works of Supererogation.*

Voluntary works,—besides, over and above God's commandments—which are called works of supererogation, cannot be taught without arrogancy and impiety. For by them men do declare that they do not only render unto God as much as they are bound to do, but that they do more for his sake than of bounden duty is required: whereas Christ saith plainly, When ye have done all that is commanded you say, We are unprofitable servants.

XII. *Of Sin after Justification.*

Not every sin willingly committed after justification is the sin against the Holy Ghost, and unpardonable. Wherefore, the grant of repentance is not to be denied to such as fall into sin, after justification; after we have received the Holy Ghost, we may depart from grace given, and fall into sin, and by the grace of God, rise again and amend our lives. And therefore they are to be condemned who say they can no more sin as long as they live here: or deny the place of forgiveness to such as truly repent.

XIII. *Entire Sanctification.*

Merely justified persons, while they do not outwardly commit sin, are nevertheless conscious of sin still remaining in the heart. They feel a natural tendency to evil, a proneness to depart from God, and cleave to the things of earth. Those that are sanctified wholly are saved from all inward sin—from evil thoughts, and evil tempers. No wrong temper, none contrary to love remains in the soul. All the thoughts, words and actions are governed by pure love.

Entire sanctification takes place subsequently to justification, and is the work of God wrought instantaneously upon the consecrated, believing soul. After a soul is cleansed from all sin, it is then fully prepared to grow in grace.

XIV.   *Future Reward and Punishment.*

God has appointed a day in which he will judge the world in righteousness by Jesus Christ according to the Gospel. The righteous shall have in heaven an inheritance incorruptible, undefiled, and that fadeth not away. The wicked shall go away into everlasting punishment, where their worm dieth not and their fire is not quenched.

XV.   *Of speaking in the Congregation in such a Tongue as the People understand.*

It is a thing plainly repugnant to the word of God, and the custom of the primitive Church, to have public prayer in the Church, or to minister the sacraments, in a tongue not understood by the people.

XVI.   *Of the Church.*

The visible Church of Christ is a congregation of faithful men, in which the pure word of God is preached, and the sacraments duly administered, according to Christ's ordinance, in all those things that of necessity are requisite to the same.

XVII.   *Of the Sacraments.*

Sacraments ordained of Christ, are not only badges or tokens of Christian men's profession; but rather they are certain signs of grace, and God's good-will toward us, by the which he doth work invisibly in us, and doth not only quicken, but also strengthen and confirm our faith in him.

XVIII.   *Of Baptism.*

Baptism is not only a sign of profession, and mark of difference, whereby Christians are distinguished from others that are not baptised; but it is also a sign of regeneration, or the new birth.   The baptism of young children is to be retained in the Church.

XIX.   *Of the Lord's Supper.*

The supper of the Lord is not merely a sign of the love that Christians ought to have among themselves one to another, but rather is a sacrament of our redemption by Christ's death; insomuch that, to such as rightly, worthily, and with faith receive the same, the bread which we break is a partaking of the body of Christ; and likewise the cup of blessing is a partaking of the blood of Christ.

Transubstantiation, or the change of the substance of bread and wine in the supper of our Lord, cannot be proved by Holy Writ, but it is repugnant to the plain words of Scripture, overthroweth the nature of a sacrament, and hath given occasion to many superstitions.

The body of Christ, is given, taken, and eaten in the supper, only after a heavenly and spiritual manner.   And the means whereby the body of Christ is received and eaten in the supper, is faith.

The sacrament of the Lord's supper was not by Christ's ordinance reserved, carried about, lifted up, or worshipped.

XX. *Of the one Oblation of Christ, finished upon the Cross.*

The offering of Christ, once made, is that perfect redemption, propitiation, and satisfaction for all the sins of the whole world, both original and actual: and there is none other satisfaction for sin but that alone. Wherefore the sacrifice of masses in the which it is said that the priest doth offer Christ for the quick and the dead, to have remission of pain or guilt, is a blasphemous fable and dangerous deceit.

XXI. *Of the Rites and Ceremonies of Churches.*

It is not necessary that rites and ceremonies should in all places be the same, or exactly alike; for they have been always different, and may be changed according to the diversity of countries, times, and men's manners, so that nothing be ordained against God's word. Whosoever, through his private judgment, willingly and purposely doth openly break the rights and ceremonies of the Church to which he belongs, which are not repugnant to the word of God, and are ordained and approved by common authority, ought to be rebuked openly, that others may fear to do the like, as one that offendeth against the common order of the Church, and woundeth the consciences of weak brethren.

Every particular Church may ordain, change, or abolish, rites and ceremonies, so that all things may be done to edification.

XXII.   *Of Christian Men's Goods.*

The riches and goods of Christians are not common, as touching the right, title, and possession of the same, as some do falsely boast. Notwithstanding, every man ought, of such things as he possesseth, liberally to give alms to the poor, according to his ability.

XXIII.   *Of a Christian Man's Oath.*

As we confess that vain and rash swearing is forbidden Christian men by our Lord Jesus Christ and James his apostle; so we judge that the Christian religion doth not prohibit, but that a man may swear when the magistrate requireth, in a cause of faith and charity, so it be done according to the prophet's teaching, in justice, judgment and truth.

SECTION II.

GENERAL RULES.

The Nature, Design, and General Rules of our United Societies.

(1) In the latter end of the year 1739, eight or ten persons came to Mr. Wesley in London, who appeared to be deeply convinced of sin, and earnestly groaning for redemptlon. They desired (as did two or three more the next day) that he would spend some time with them in prayer, and advise them how to flee from the wrath to come; which they saw continually hanging over their heads. That he might have more time for this great work, he appointed a day when they might all come together, which from thenceforward they did every week, namely, on *Thursday*, in the evening. For these, and as many more as desired to join with them, (for their number increased daily,) he gave those advices from time to time which he judged most needful for them; and they always concluded their meeting with prayer suited to their several necessities.

(2) This was the rise of the UNITED SOCIETY, *first in Europe*, and then in *America*. Such a society is no other than "*a company of men* having the form and seeking the power of *godliness, united in order to pray together, to receive the word of exhortation, and to watch over one another*

in love, that they may help each other to work out their salvation."

(3) That it may the more easily be discerned whether they are indeed working out their own salvation, each society is divided into smaller companies, called classes, according to their respective places of abode. There are about twelve persons in a class; one of whom is styled *the leader.* It is his duty,

I. To see each person in his class once a week at least; in order,

1. To inquire how their souls prosper.

2. To advise, reprove, comfort or exhort, as occasion may require.

3. To receive what they are willing to give toward the relief of the preacher, church and poor.*

II. To meet the minister and the stewards of the society once a week; in order,

1. To inform the minister of any that are sick, or of any that walk disorderly, and will not be reproved.

2. To pay the stewards what they have have received of their several classes in the week preceding.

(4) There is only one condition previously required of those who desire admission into these societies, "a desire to flee from the wrath to

---

* This part refers to towns and cities; where the poor are generally numerous, and church expenses considerable.

come, and to be saved from their sins." But wherever this is really fixed in the soul, it will be shown by its fruits. It is therefore expected of all who continue therein, that they should continue to evidence their desire of salvation,

First, By doing no harm, by avoiding evil of every kind, especially that which is most generally practiced; such as,

The taking of the name of God in vain.

The profaning the day of the Lord, either by doing ordinary work therein, or by buying or selling.

Drunkenness, buying or selling spirituous liquors, or drinking them, unless in cases of extreme necessity.

The buying, selling, or holding of a human being as a slave.

Fighting, quarrelling, brawling, brother *going to law* with brother; returning evil for evil; or railing for railing; the *using many words* in buying or selling.

The buying or selling goods that have not paid the duty.

The *giving or taking things on usury*, i. e. unlawful interest.

Uncharitable or *unprofitable* conversation; particularly speaking evil of magistrates or ministers.

Doing to others as we would not they should do unto us.

Doing what we know is not for the glory of God; as

The putting on of gold or costly apparel.

The *taking such diversions* as cannot be used in the name of the Lord Jesus.

The *singing* those *songs,* or *reading* those *books,* which do not tend to the knowledge or love of God.

Softness and needless self-indulgence.

Laying up treasure upon earth.

Borrowing without a probability of paying; or taking up goods without a probability of paying for them.

(5) It is expected of all who continue in these societies, that they should continue to evidence their desire of salvation,

Secondly, By doing good, by being in every kind merciful after their power, as they have opportunity, doing good of every possible sort, and as far as possible, to all men.

To their bodies, of the ability which God giveth, by giving food to the hungry, by clothing the naked, by visiting or helping them that are sick or in prison.

To their souls, by instructing, reproving, or exhorting all we have any intercourse with; trampling under foot that enthusiastic doctrine, that "we are not to do good unless *our hearts be free to it.*"

By doing good, especially to them that are of the household of faith, or groaning so to be; employing them preferably to others, buying one of another, helping each other in business; and so much the more because the world will love its own, and them *only*.

By all possible *diligence* and *frugality*, that the gospel be not blamed.

By running with patience the race which is set before them, *denying themselves and taking up their cross daily;* submitting to bear the reproach of Christ, to be as the filth and offscouring of the world; and looking that men should say *all manner of evil of them falsely for the Lord's sake.*

(6) It is expected of all who desire to continue in these societies, that they should continue to evidence their desire of salvation,

Thirdly, By attending upon all the ordinances of God: such are,

The public worship of God:

The ministry of the word, either read or expounded:

The supper of the Lord:

Family and private prayer:

Searching the Scriptures, and

Fasting or Abstinence.

(7) These are the general rules of our societies: all of which we are taught of God to observe, even in his written word, which is the only rule, and the sufficient rule both of our faith and practice. And all these we know his Spirit writes on truly awakened hearts. If there be any among us who observe them not, who habitually break any of them, let it be

known unto them who watch over that soul, as they who must give an account. We will admonish him of the error of his ways. We will bear with him for a season. But if then he repent not, he hath no more place among us. We have delivered our own souls.

SECTION III.

Of Receiving Members into the Church.

1. Let none be admitted on probation, until they give satisfactory evidence of Scriptural conversion, and are recommended by some member of our Church.

2. Let none be received into full connection, unless they give evidence of a renewed heart, and until they are recommended by their leader, and have met in class six months on probation, have been baptized, and can give satisfactory answers to the following questions which shall be proposed to them before the society :

1. Have you the witness of THE SPIRIT that you are a child of God ?

2. Have you that perfect love which casteth out fear? If not will you diligently seek until you obtain it?

3. Is it your purpose to devote yourself the remainder of your life wholly to the service of God, doing good to your fellow men and working out your own salvation with fear and trembling?

4. Will you forever lay aside all superfluous ornaments, and adorn yourself in modest apparel, with shame-facedness and sobriety, not with broidered hair, or gold or pearls, or costly array, but which becometh those professing godliness with good works?

5. Will you abstain from connection with all secret societies, keeping yourself free to follow the will of the Lord in all things?

6. Do you subscribe to our articles of religion, our general rules, and our Discipline, and are you willing to be governed by the same?

7. Have you Christian fellowship and love for the members of this society, and will you assist them as God shall give you ability in carrying on the work of the Lord?

The person giving affirmative answers to the above questions shall, with the consent of three-fourths of all the numbers present at a society meeting, be admitted to all the privileges of a member.

CHAPTER II.

OF THE CONVENTIONS.

SECTION I.

Of our Deportment at the Conventions.

It is desired that all things be considered on on these occasions as in the immediate presence of God; that every person speak freely whatever is in his heart.

Quest. How may we best improve our time at the Conventions?

Answ. 1. While we are conversing, let us have an especial care to set God always before us.

2. In the intermediate hours, let us redeem all the time we can for private exercises.

3. Therein let us give ourselves to prayer for one another, and for a blessing on our labor.

SECTION II.

Of the General Convention.

1. The General Convention shall be composed of an equal number of clerical and lay delegates belonging to the Free Methodist Church, to be appointed by the Annual Conventions, at their respective sessions next preceding the session of the General Convention. Each Annual Convention shall be entitled to one lay and one ministerial delegate; and an additional one of each kind for every ten preachers belonging to it in full connection. The traveling preachers in full connection, in each of the Annual Conventions, and the lay members of the same, shall elect from their own number the delegates to which they are respectively entitled.

2. The General Convention shall meet on the second Wednesday of October, 1862, at St.

Charles, Ills., and once in four years thereafter, at such place as it may designate.

3. At all times when the General Convention shall be in session, it shall take two-thirds of all the delegates who shall attend and be enrolled, to constitute a quorum for transacting business.

4. Each General Convention shall elect one or more Superintendents, and a Secretary, by ballot.

5. The members of the General Convention shall deliberate and vote as one body; nevertheless, upon a call of one-fourth of the members, the house shall divide, and it shall require a majority of the ministerial, and a majority of the lay delegates present, to pass any vote or transact any business.

6. The General Convention shall have full powers to make rules and regulations for our Church, under the following limitations and restrictions:

1. The General Convention shall not revoke, alter, or change our articles of religion, nor the general rules of the United Societies, nor establish any new standards or rules of doctrine, contrary to our present existing and established standards of doctrine.

2. They shall not change or alter any part or rule of our government, so as to do away with lay delegation or an itinerant ministry, or the Free Seat system in all our Churches.

3. They shall not have power to deprive our preachers or members of the right of trial by an

impartial Committee, and of an appeal. Provided, nevertheless, that upon the concurrent recommendation of three-fourths of all the members of the several Annual Conventions, who shall be present and vote on such recommendation, then a majority of two-thirds of the General Convention succeeding shall suffice to alter any of the above restrictions except the last; and also, whenever such alteration, or alterations, shall have been first recommended by two-thirds of the General Convention so soon as three-fourths of the members of all the Annual Conventions shall have concurred as aforesaid, such alteration or alterations shall take effect.

SECTION III.

Of the Annual Conventions.

1. The Annual Conventions shall be composed of all the traveling and superannuated preachers in full connection, who have been duly received within its bounds, and of an equal number of lay delegates, elected as follows: Each circuit or station shall have an Annual Meeting within three months preceding the session of the Annual Convention, at which the members of the Church in full connection belonging to that circuit or station, twenty years old and upwards, shall elect by ballot, one at least of their number to represent them in the Annual Convention. The members of each circuit shall be entitled to

one delegate for every traveling preacher on their circuit belonging to the Annual Convention.

2. Each Annual Convention shall appoint the place, and with the concurrence of the President the time of its own sessions.

3. They shall elect a Secretary who shall record in a suitable book the proceedings of the Annual Convention, which record shall be sent to the General Convention for their examination.

4. The ministers and laymen composing the Annual Convention shall deliberate and vote as one body; but at the call of one-fourth of all the members present, the house shall divide, and the ministers and laymen vote separately; and it shall require a majority of both branches to constitute a vote of the Convention.

5. The territory embraced by each Annual Convention shall be divided into districts, and over each of these one of the traveling elders shall be appointed by the Annual Convention as Chairman.

6. The President of the Annual Convention, with the Chairmen of the several districts, and an equal number of laymen to be elected by ballot the first day of the session, shall constitute a stationing committee, (of which the President of the Convention shall be Chairman, having a casting vote,) whose duty it shall be to appoint the preachers to their several fields of labor; provided that no preacher shall be ap-

pointed to the same circuit or station more than two years in succession, nor more than two years out of six.

7. Each Annual Convention shall inquire—

1. What preachers are admitted on trial?

2. Who remain on trial?

3. Who are admitted into full connexion?

4. Who are the Deacons?

5. Who have been elected and ordained Elders this year?

6. Who have located this year?

7. Who are the superannuated or worn-out preachers?

8. Who have been expelled from the connexion this year?

9. Who have withdrawn from the connexion this year?

10. Are all the preachers blameless in life and conversation?

11. Who have died this year?

12. What is the number of Church members?

Amount collected for superannuated preachers?

Amount collected for the Missionary Society?

Amount collected for the American Bible Society?

Number of Sunday Schools?

Number of officers and teachers?

Number of scholars?

Number of volumes in library?

13. What amounts are necessary for the su-

perannuated preachers, and the widows and
orphans of preachers, and to make up the defi-
ciencies of those who have not obtained their
regular allowance on the circuits?

14. What has been collected on the foregoing
accounts, and how has it been applied?

15. Where are the preachers stationed this
year?

16. Where and when shall our next Convention be held?

Quest. Is there are any other business to be
done in the Annual Convention?

Answ. The electing and ordaining of Deacons
and Elders.

SECTON IV.

Of the Quarterly Conventions.

1. The Quarterly Convention shall be composed of all the traveling and local preachers,
exhorters, stewards, and leaders of the district.

2. Four sessions of the Quarterly Convention
shall be held each year in connection with the
General Quarterly Meetings, at such times and
places as it may designate.

3. The Chairman of the district shall be
President of the Quarterly Convention, and in
his absence a President pro tem shall be elected
by the members present.

4. A Secretary shall be appointed by the
Quarterly Convention, who shall keep a faithful
record of its proceedings.

5. The Quarterly Convention shall hear complaints and try appeals, grant and renew licences to preach, and recommend suitable persons to the Annual Convention to be employed as traveling preachers. No person shall be licensed to preach until he has first been recommended by the Society of which he is a member, or the official meeting of said Society, and until he has first been examined by the Quarterly Convention in regard to his piety, his soundness in doctrine, his gifts and his usefulness. Let none be licensed until satisfactory answers are given to all the questions found in the section, " *Of the trial of those who think they are moved by the Holy Ghost to preach.*" The Quarterly Convention, shall also in connection with the Chairman of the District, appoint and hold Camp Meetings as the interests of the cause of God may require.

CHAPTER III.

SECTION I.

OF OFFICERS AND MINISTERS.

Of the General Superintendents.

1. The General Convention shall elect one or more Traveling Elders as General Superintendents to remain in office during the four years following, or until the next session of the General Convention.

2. It shall be the duty of the Superintendents to travel through the connection at large; to oversee the spiritual and temporal interests of our Church, and to labor to promote its purity, peace and prosperity; to establish new Churches, to preside at the General and Annual Conventions, and to decide all questions of law therein, subject to an appeal to the respective Conventions.

3. The Superintendents shall be amenable to the General Convention for the discharge of their official duties, and for their Christian conduct, to the Annual Conventions to which they respectively belong.

SECTION II.

Of the Chairmen of Districts.

It shall be the duty of the Chairman of a district—

1. To look after the spiritual and temporal interests of our Church within his district, and to take the general oversight of the work on his district, according to the discipline, so far as his duty to the circuit to which he is appointed will permit.

2. To see that every part of the discipline is duly enforced.

3. To visit every circuit or station on his district whenever he may judge it expedient. The Chairman is especially directed and required to visit any circuit or station in his district, when

so requested by the preacher in charge, or by the official board, in case of any dispute or difficulty, or any emergency that may arise. The circuit or station sending for him shall pay his traveling expenses.

4. To hold four General Quarterly Meetings in his district during each year.

5. To change, receive, and suspend Preachers in his district in the intervals of the Convention, and in the absence of the Superintendent. Provided, nevertheless, he shall not change any preacher contrary to his wishes, unless by the request of two-thirds of the members of the circuit or station.

6. To give the Superintendent all necessary information of the state of his district.

7. The Chairman shall not have power to employ a preacher that has been rejected by the Annual Convention without permission by said Convention.

8. No Chairman shall preside over the same district more than four years in succession.

9. The Chairman shall be supported by the circuit or station to which he is appointed.

SECTION III.

Of the Election and Ordination of Traveling Elders, and of their Duty.

Quest. 1. How is an Elder constituted?

Answ. By the election of a majority of the

Annual Convention, and by the laying on of the hands of some of the Elders that are present.

Quest. 2. What is the duty of a Traveling Elder?

Answ. 1. To administer baptism and the Lord's supper, and to perform the office of matrimony, and all parts of divine worship.

2. To do all the duties of a traveling preacher.

No Elder that ceases to travel, without the consent of the Annual Conference, certified under the hand of the President of the Conference, except in case of sickness, debility, or other unavoidable circumstances, shall on any account exercise the peculiar functions of his office, or even be allowed to preach among us: *nevertheless*, the final determination in all such cases is with the Annual Conference.

SECTION IV.

Of the Election and Ordination of Traveling Deacons, and of their Duty.

Quest. 1. How is a Traveling Deacon constituted?

Answ. By the election of a majority of the Annual Conference, and the laying on of the hands of some of the Elders present.

Quest. 2. What is the duty of a Traveling Deacon?

Answ. 1. To baptise and perform the office of matrimony, in the absence of the Elder.

2. To assist the Elder in administering the Lord's supper.

3. To do all the duties of a traveling preacher.

Quest. 3. What shall be the time of probation of a Traveling Deacon for the office of an Elder?

Answ. Every Traveling Deacon shall exercise that office for two years, before he be eligible to the office of Elder; except in the case of missions, when the Annual Conventions shall have authority to elect for the Elder's office sooner, if they judge it expedient.

No Deacon who ceases to travel without the consent of the Annual Convention certified under the hand of the President of the Convention, except in case of sickness, debility or other unavoidable circumstances, shall on any account exercise the peculiar functions of his office, or even be allowed to preach among us; *nevertheless*, the final determination in all such cases is with the Annual Convention.

SECTION V.

Of the Reception of Preachers from other Denominations.

Quest. How shall we receive those ministers who may offer to unite with us from other Christian Churches?

Answ. Those ministers of other evangelical Churches, who may desire to unite with our

Church, whether as local or itinerant, may be received according to our usages, on condition of their taking upon them our ordination vows. without the reimposition of hands, giving satis-faction to an Annual Convention of their being in orders, and of their agreement with us in doctrine, discipline, government and usages: *provided*, the Convention is also satisfied with their gifts, graces and usefulness.

SECTION VI.

Of the Examination of those who 'think they are moved by the Holy Ghost to preach.

Quest. How shall we try those who profess to be moved by the Holy Ghost to preach?

Answ. 1. Let the following questions be asked, namely:—Do they know God as a pardoning God? Have they the love of God abiding in them? Do they desire nothing but God? And are they holy in all manner of conversation?

2. Have they gifts (as well as grace) for the work? Have they (in some tolerable de-gree) a clear, sound understanding, a right judgment in the things of God, a just concep-tion of salvation by faith? And has God given them any degree of utterance? Do they speak justly, readily, clearly?

3. Have they fruit? Are any truly convinced of sin, and converted to God by their preaching?

As long as these three marks concur in any

one, we believe he is called of God to preach. These we receive as sufficient proof that he is moved by the Holy Ghost.

SECTION VII.

Of the Reception of Preachers.

Quest. 1. How shall a preacher be received on trial?

Answ. By the Annual Convention, after passing a satisfactory examination as prescribed in the last section, and in the course of study laid down for probationers, and having been duly recommended by a Quarterly Convention.

Quest. 2. How shall a traveling preacher be received into full connexion?

Answ. 1. He must give satisfactory answers to the following questions, namely: Have you faith in Christ? Have you the present assurance of sins forgiven? Do you believe in Christian perfection? Have you attained to this rich experience in your own heart? (If not) Are you groaning after it? Are you resolved to devote yourself wholly to God and his work? Do you know the General Rules? Do you keep them? Do you constantly attend the sacrament? Have you read our Discipline? Are you willing to conform to it? Have you considered the rules of a preacher? Will you keep them for conscience' sake? Are you determined to employ all your time in the work of

God? Will you endeavor not to speak too long nor too loud? Will you diligently instruct the children in every place? Will you visit from house to house? Will you recommend fasting or abstinence, both by precept and example? Are you in debt? Do you use snuff, tobacco or drams?

Answ. 2. He must have been employed in the regular itinerant work for two successive years, after he was received on trial by the Annual Convention.

Answ. 3. He must pass a satisfactory examination in the prescribed course of study.

SECTION VIII.

Of the Rules for a Preacher's Conduct.

Quest. 1. What are the directions given to a Preacher?

Answ. 1. Be diligent. Never be unemployed; never be triflingly employed. Never trifle away time; neither spend any more time at any place than is strictly necessary.

2. Be serious. Let your motto be *Holiness to the Lord.* Avoid all lightness, jesting and foolish talking.

3. Converse sparingly, and conduct yourself prudently with women. 1 Tim. v. 2.

4. Take no step toward marriage without first consulting with your brethren.

5. Believe evil of no one without good evi-

dence; unless you see it done, take heed how
you credit it. Put the best construction on everything. You know the judge is always supposed to be on the prisoner's side.

6. Speak evil of no one; because your word,
especially, would eat as doth a canker. Keep
your thoughts within your own breast, till you
come to the person concerned.

7. Tell every one under your care what you
think wrong in his conduct and temper, and
that lovingly and plainly as soon as may be;
else it will fester in your heart. Make all haste
to cast the fire out of your bosom.

8. Avoid all affectation. A preacher of the
gospel is the servant of all.

9. Be ashamed of nothing but sin.

10. Be punctual, Do everything exactly at
the time. And do not mend our rules, but keep
them; not for wrath, but conscience' sake.

11. You have nothing to do but to save souls:
therefore spend and be spent in this work; and
go always not only to those that want you, but
to those that want you most.

Observe! it is not your business only to preach
so many times, and to take care of this or that
society; but to save as many as you can; to
bring as many sinners as you can to repentance,
and with all your power to build them up in
that holiness without which they cannot see the
Lord. And remember!—a Methodist Preacher
is to mind every point, great and small, in the

Methodist Discipline! Therefore you will need to exercise all the sense and grace you have.

12. Act in all things not according to your own will, but as a son in the gospel. As such it is your duty to employ your time in the manner in which we direct: in preaching, and visiting from house to house; in reading, meditation, and prayer. Above all if you labor with us in the Lord's vineyard, it is needful you should do that part of the work which we advise, at those times and places which we judge most for his glory.

Quest. 2. Are there any smaller advices which might be of use to us?

Answ. Perhaps these: 1. Be sure never to disappoint a congregation. 2. Begin at the time appointed. 3. Let your whole deportment be serious, weighty, and solemn. 4. Always suit your subject to your audience. 5. Choose the plainest texts you can. 6. Take care not to ramble, but keep to your text, and make out what you take in hand. 7. Take care of anything awkward or affected, either in your gesture, phrase, or pronunciation. 8. Do not usually pray *extempore*, above eight or ten minutes (at most) without intermission. 9. Frequently read and enlarge upon a portion of Scripture; and let young preachers often exhort without taking a text. 10. Always avail yourself of the great festivals, by preaching on the occasion.

SECTION IX.

Of the Duty of Preachers to God, themselves, and one another.

Quest. 1. What is the duty of a preacher?

Answ. 1. To preach.

2. To meet the societies and classes.

3. To visit the sick.

4. To preach out of doors wherever an attentive congregation can be found.

Quest. 2. How shall a preacher be qualified for his charge?

Answ. By walking closely with God, and having his work greatly at heart; and by understanding and loving discipline, ours in particular.

Quest. 3. Do we sufficiently watch over each other?

Answ. We do not. Should we not frequently ask each other, Do you walk closely with God? Have you now fellowship with the Father and the Son? At what hour do you rise? Do you punctually observe the morning and evening hours of retirement? Do you spend the day in the manner which the Convention advises? Do you converse seriously, usefully, and closely? To be more particular: Do you use all the means of grace yourself, and enforce the use of them on all other persons? They are either instituted or prudential.

I. The instituted are,

1. Prayer; private, family, and public: consisting of deprecation, petition, intercession and thanksgiving. Do you use each of these? Do you forecast daily, wherever you are, to secure time for private devotion? Do you practice it every where? Do you ask everywhere, Have you family prayer? Do you ask individuals, Do you use private prayer every morning and evening in particular?

2. Searching the Scriptures, by

(1) Reading: constantly, some part of every day; regularly, all the Bible in order; carefully, with notes; seriously, with prayer before and after; fruitfully, immediately practising what you learn there?

(2) Meditating: At set times? By rule?

(3) Hearing: Every opportunity? With prayer, before, at, after? Have you a Bible always about you?

3. The Lord's supper: Do you use this at every opportunity? With solemn prayer before? With earnest and deliberate self-devotion?

4. Fasting: Do you use as much abstinence and fasting every week, as your health, strength, and labor will permit?

5. Christian conference: Are you convinced how important and difficult it is to order your conversation aright? Is it always in grace? Seasoned with salt? Meet to minister grace to the hearers? Do you not converse too long at

a time? Is not an hour commonly enough? Would it not be well always to have a determined end in view? And to pray before and after it?

II. Prudential means we may use either as Christians, as Methodists, or as preachers.

1. As Christians: What particular rules have you in order to grow in grace? What arts of holy living?

2. As Methodists: Do you never miss your class?

3. As Preachers: Have you thoroughly considered your duty? And do you make a conscience of executing every part of it? Do you meet every society and their leaders?

These means may be used without fruit. But there are some means which cannot: namely, watching, denying ourselves, taking up our cross, exercise of the presence of God.

1. Do you steadily watch against the world? Yourself? Your besetting sin?

2. Do you deny yourself every useless pleasuse of sense? Imagination? Honor? Are you temperate in all things? Instance in food: (1) Do you use only that kind and that degree which is best both for body and soul? Do you see the necessity of this? (2) Do you eat no more at each meal than is necessary? Are you not heavy or drowsy after dinner? (3) Do you use only that kind, and that degree of drink, which is best both for your body and soul? (4)

Do you choose and use water for your common drink? And only take wine medicinally or sacramentally?

3. Wherein do you take up your cross daily? Do you cheerfully bear your cross, however grievous of nature, as a gift of God, and labor to profit thereby?

4. Do you endeavor to set God always before you? To see his eye continually fixed upon you? Never can you use these means but a blessing will ensue. And the more you use them, the more you will grow in grace.

SECTION X.

Of the Duties of those who have the Charge of Circuits or Stations.

Quest. 1. What are the duties of the preacher who has the special charge of a circuit?

Answ. 1. To see that the other preachers in his circuit behave well, and want nothing.

2. To nominate all the leaders subject to confirmation by the class, and to examine each of the leaders with all possible exactness, at least once a quarter, concerning his method of leading his class.

3. To hold watch-nights, and love-feasts, and to see that the sacrament is administered at least once in three months.

4. To take care that every society be duly supplied with books.

5. To take an exact account of all the members in society in their respective circuits and stations, keeping the names of all local elders, deacons, and preachers, properly distinguished, and deliver such account to the Annual Convention that their number may be printed in the minutes.

6. To give an account of his circuit every quarter to the Chairman of the District.

7. To report to the Society at least once a quarter, the names of those who have been received into the Church or excluded therefrom during the quarter: also the names of those who have been received or dismissed by certificate, and of those who have died or have withdrawn from the Church.

Quest. 2. What other directions shall we give him?

Answ. Several.

1. To take a regular catalogue of the societies in towns and cities, as they live in the streets.

2. To leave his successor a particular account of the circuit, including an account of the subscribers for our periodicals.

3. To enforce vigorously, but calmly, all the rules of the society.

4. As soon as there are four believers in any place to put them into a class.

5. To warn all from time to time, that none are to remove from one circuit to another, with-

out a note of recommendation from the preacher of the circuit in these words:—" *A. B., the bearer, has been an acceptable member of the Free Methodist Church.*" And to inform them that without such a certificate, they will not be received into the Church in other places.

6. To recommend everywhere decency and cleanliness.

7. To read the rules of the society, with the aid of the other preachers, once a year in every congregation, and once a quarter in every society.

8. The preacher who has the charge of a circuit shall appoint prayer meetings wherever he can in his circuit.

9. He shall take care that a fast be held in every society in his circuit, on the Friday preceding every quarterly meeting : and that a memorandum of it be written on all the class papers.

N. B. The preachers who have the oversight of circuits are required to execute all our rules fully and strenuously against all frauds, and particularly against dishonest insolvencies; suffering none to remain in our Church on any account who are found guilty of any fraud.

Quest. 3. What can be done to supply the circuits during the sittings of the Conventions.

Answ. 1. Let all the appointments stand according to the plan of the circuit.

2. Engage as many local preachers and exhorters as will supply them; and let them be paid for their time in proportion to the allowance of the traveling preachers.

3. If preachers and exhorters cannot attend, let some person of ability be appointed in every society, to sing, pray, and read one of Mr. Wesley's sermons.

4. But if that cannot be done, let there be prayer meetings.

SECTION XI.

Of the Matter and Manner of Preaching.

Quest. 1. What is the best general method of preaching?

Answ. 1. To convince: 2. To offer Christ: 3. To invite: 4. To build up: And to do this in some measure in every sermon.

Quest. 2. What is the most effectual way of preaching Christ?

Answ. The most effectual way of preaching Christ is, to preach him in all his offices; and to declare his law, as well as his gospel, both to believers and unbelievers. Let us strongly and closely insist upon inward and outward holiness in all its branches.

SECTION XII.

Rules by which we should continue, or desist from Preaching at any Place.

Quest. 1. Is it advisable for us to preach in as many places as we can, without forming any societies?

Answ. By no means. We have made the trial in various places; and that for a considerable length of time. But all the seed has fallen by the way-side. There is scarcely any fruit remaining.

Quest. 2. Where should we endeavor to preach most?

Answ. 1. Where there is the greatest number of quiet and willing hearers.

2. Where there is most fruit.

Quest. 3. Ought we not diligently to observe in what places God is pleased at any time to pour out his Spirit more abundantly?

Answ. We ought: and at that time to send more laborers than usual into that part of the harvest.

SECTION XIII.

Of Visiting from House to House, Guarding against those things that are so common to Professors, and Enforcing Practical Religion.

Quest. 1. How can we further assist those under our care?

Answ. By instructing them at their own houses. What unspeakable need is there of this! The world says, " *The Methodists are no better than other people.*" This is not true in the general: but, 1. Personal religion, either towards God or man, is too superficial among us. We can but just touch on a few particulars.

How little faith is there among us! How little
communion with God, how little living in heaven,
walking in eternity, deadness to every creature!
How much love of the world! Desire of pleas-
ure, of ease, of getting money! How little
brotherly love! What continual judging one
another! What gossipping, evil-speaking, tale-
bearing! What want of moral honesty! To
instance only one particular; who does as he
would be done by in buying and selling?

2. Family religion is wanting in many branches. And what avails public preaching alone,
though we could preach like angels? We must,
yea, every traveling preacher must, instruct the
people from house to house. Till this be done,
and that in good earnest, Methodists will be no
better.

Our religion is not sufficiently deep, universal,
uniform; but superficial, partial, uneven. It
will be so till we spend half as much time in
this visiting, as we now do in talking uselessly.
Can we find a better method of doing this than
Mr. Baxter's. If not, let us adopt it without
delay. His whole tract, entitled, *The Reformed
Pastor*, is well worth a careful perusal. Speaking of this visiting from house to house, he says,
"We shall find many hindrances, both in ourselves and the people."

1. In ourselves there is much dullness and la-
ziness, so that there will be much ado to get us
to be faithful in the work.

2. We have a base, man-pleasing temper, so that we let them perish rather than lose their love; we let them go quietly to hell lest we should offend them.

3. Some of us have a foolish bashfulness. We know not how to begin, and blush to contradict the devil.

4. But the greater hindrance is weakness of faith. Our whole motion is weak, because the spring of it is weak.

5. Lastly, we are unskillful in the work. How few know how to deal with men, so as to get within them, and suit all our discourse to their several conditions and tempers: to choose the fittest subjects, and follow them with a holy mixture of seriousness, terror, love, and meekness !

But undoubtedly this private application is implied in those solemn words of the apostle; "I charge thee before God and the Lord Jesus Christ, who shall judge the quick and the dead at his appearing, preach the word: be instant in season, out of season: reprove, rebuke, exhort, with all long-suffering."

O, brethren, if we could but set this work on foot in all our societies, and prosecute it zealously, what glory would redound to God! If the common lukewarmness were banished, and every shop, and every house, busied in speaking of the word and works of God, surely God would dwell in our habitations, and make us his delight.

And this is absolutely necessary to the welfare of our people, some of whom neither repent nor believe to this day. Look round, and see how many of them are still in apparent danger of damnation. And how can you walk and talk, and be merry with such people, when you know their case? When you look them in the face, you should break forth into tears, as the prophet did when he looked upon Hazael, and then set on them with the most vehement exhortations. O, for God's sake, and the sake of poor souls, bestir yourselves, and spare no pains that may conduce to their salvation !

What cause have we to bleed before the Lord that we have so long neglected this good work! If we had but engaged in it sooner, how many more might have been brought to Christ! And how much holier and happier might our societies have been before now! And why might we not have done it sooner? There were many hindrances; and so there always will be. But the greatest hindrance is in ourselves, in our littleness of faith and love.

But it is objected, I. "This will take up so much time, we shall not have leisure to follow our studies." We answer, 1. Gaining knowledge is a good thing, but saving souls is better. 2. By this very thing you will gain the most excellent knowledge, that of God and eternity. 3. You will have time for gaining other knowledge too. Only sleep no more than you need; "and never be idle, or triflingly employed." But, 4. If you can do but one, let your studies alone. We ought to throw by all the libraries in the world, rather than be guilty of the loss of one soul.

It is objected, II. "The people will not submit to it." If some will not others will. And the success with them will repay all your labor. O let us herein follow the example of St. Paul! 1. For our general business, *Serving the Lord with all humility of mind:* 2. Our special work, *Take heed to yourselves and to all the flock:* 3. Our doctrine, *Repentance toward God, and faith toward our Lord Jesus Christ:* 4. The place, *I have taught you publicly, and from house to house:* 5. The object and manner of teaching, *I cease not to warn every one night and day, with tears:* 6. His innocence and self-denial herein, *I have coveted no man's silver or gold:* 7. His patience, *Neither count I my life dear unto myself:* And among all other motives, let these be ever before our eyes: 1. *The Church which he hath purchased with his own blood:* 2. *Grievious wolves shall enter in: yea, of yourselves shall men arise, speaking perverse things.*

Write this upon your hearts, and it will do you more good than twenty years study. Then you will have no time to spare; you will have work enough. Then likewise no preacher will stay with us who is as salt that has lost its savour. For to such this employment will be mere drudgery. And in order to it, you will

have need of all the knowledge you can procure,
and grace you can attain.

The sum is, Go into every house in course,
and teach every one therein, young and old to
be Christians inwardly and outwardly; make every particular plain to their understandings; fix
it in their minds; write it on their hearts.   In
order to this there must be line upon line, precept upon precept.   What patience, what love,
what knowledge, is requisite for this!   We
must needs do this, were it only to avoid idleness.   Do we not loiter away many hours in
every week?   Each try himself; no idleness is
consistent with a growth in grace.   Nay, without exactness in redeeming time, you cannot
retain the grace you receive in justification.

Quest. 2. Why are we not more holy?   Why
do we not live in eternity?   Walk with God all
the day long?   Why are we not we all devoted
to good?   Breathing the whole spirit of missionaries?

Answ. Chiefly because we are enthusiasts;
looking for the end without using the means.
To touch only upon two or three instances:—
Who of us rises at four, or even at five, when
we do not preach?   Do we know the obligation
and benefit of fasting or abstinence?   How often do we practice it?   The neglect of this
alone is sufficient to account for our feebleness
and faintness of spirit.   We are continually
grieving the Holy Spirit of God by the habitual

neglect of a plain duty.   Let us amend from this
hour.

Quest. How shall we guard against Sabbath
breaking, evil-speaking, unprofitable conversation, lightness, expensiveness or gayety of apparel, and contracting debts without due care to
discharge them ?

Answ. 1. Let us preach expressly on each of
these heads. 2. Read in every society the sermon on evil-speaking. 3. Let the leaders closely
examine and exhort every person to put away
the accursed thing. 4. Let the preachers warn
every society that none who is guilty herein can
remain with us. 5. Extirpate out of our Church
buying or selling goods which have not paid the
duty laid upon them by government. Let none
remain with us who will not totally abstain from
this evil in every kind and degree. Extirpate
bribery, receiving anything, directly or indirectly,
for voting at any election. Show no respect to
persons herein, but expel all that touch the accursed thing. And strongly advise our people
to discountenance all treats given by candidates
before or at elections, and not to be partakers,
in any respect of such iniquitous practices.

SECTION XIV.

*Of Sunday Schools and the Religious Instruction
of Children.*

Quest. 1. What shall we do for the moral and
religious instruction of the children ?

Answ. 1. It shall be the special duty of preachers having charge of circuits or stations, with the aid of the other preachers, to form Sunday schools in all our congregations where ten children can be collected for that purpose, and to engage the co-operation of as many of our members as they can; to visit the schools as often as practicable; to preach on the subject of Sunday schools, and religious instruction in each congregation at least once in six months; and to form Bible classes wherever they can for the instruction of larger children and youth, and where they cannot superintend them personally, to see that suitable teachers are provided for that purpose.

2. It shall also be the duty of preachers to enforce faithfully upon parents and Sunday-school teachers the great importance of instructing children in the doctrines and duties of our holy religion; to see that our catechisms be used as extensively as possible, both in our Sunday schools and families; to preach to the children and publicly catechise them in the Sunday schools, and at special meetings appointed for that purpose.

3. It shall be the duty of every preacher in his pastoral visits, to pay special attention to the children, speaking to them personally and kindly on the subject of experimental and practical godliness, according to their capacity, pray earnestly for them, and diligently instruct

and exhort all parents to dedicate their children to the Lord, in baptism, as early as convenient.

4. Each preacher in charge shall lay before the Quarterly Conference, to be entered on its Journal, the number and state of the Sunday schools and Bible classes in his charge, and the extent to which he has preached to the children and catechised them, and make the required report on Sunday schools to his Annual Convention.

SECTION XV.

Of employing our Time profitably, when we are not Traveling, or engaged in Public Exercises.

Quest. 1. What general method of employing our time shall we advise?

Answ. We advise you, 1. As often as possible to rise at four. 2. From four to five in the morning, and from five to six in the evening, to meditate, pray, and read the Scriptures with notes, and the closely practical parts of what Mr. Wesley has published. 3. From six in the morning till twelve, (allowing an hour for breakfast,) read, with much prayer, some of our best religious tracts.

Quest. 2. Why is it that the people under our care are not better?

Answ. Other reasons may concur, but the chief is, because we are not more knowing and more holy.

4

Quest. 3. But why are we not more knowing?

Answ. Because we are idle. We forget our first rule, "Be diligent. Never be unemployed. Never be triflingly employed. Neither spend any more time at any place than is strictly necessary." We fear there is altogether a fault in this matter, and that few of us are clear. Which of us spend as many hours a day in God's work as we did formerly in man's work? We talk,—talk or read what comes next to hand. We must, absolutely must, cure this evil, or betray the cause of God. But how? 1. Read the most useful books, and that regularly and constantly. 2. Steadily spend all the morning in this employment, or at least five hours in the four and twenty. "But I have no taste for reading." Contract a taste for it by use, or return to your former employment. "But I have no books." Be diligent to spread the books, and you will have the use of them.

SECTION XVI.

Of the necessity of Union among ourselves.

Let us be deeply sensible (from what we have known) of the evil of a division in principle, spirit, or practice, and the dreadful consequences to ourselves and others. If we are united, what can stand before us? If we divide, we shall destroy ourselves, the work of God, and the souls of our people.

Quest. What can be done in order to a closer union with each other?

Answ. 1. Let us be deeply convinced of the absolute necessity of it.

2. Pray earnestly for, and speak freely to, each other.

3. When we meet, let us never part without prayer.

4. Take great care not to despise each other's gifts.

5. Never speak lightly of each other.

6. Let us defend each other's character in everything so far as is consistent with truth.

7. Labor in honor each to prefer the other before himself.

8. We recommend a serious perusal of *The Causes, Evils, and Cures of Heart and Church Divisions.*

SECTION XVII.

Local Preachers.

Quest. What directions shall be given concerning local preachers?

1. The Quarterly Convention shall take cognizance of all the local preachers in the circuit or station, and shall enquire into the gifts, labors and usefulness of each preacher by name.

2. A licensed local preacher shall be eligible to the office of a Deacon, after he has preached four years from the time he received a regular

license, and has obtained a recommendation from the Quarterly Convention, after proper examination.

3. A local Deacon shall be eligible to the office of an Elder, after he has preached four years from the time he was ordained a Deacon, and has obtained a recommendation from the Quarterly Convention of which he is a member, certifying his qualifications in doctrine, discipline, talents, and usefulness, signed by the President and Secretary.

4. Every local Elder, Deacon, or Preacher shall be amenable to the Quarterly Convention where he belongs, for his Christian character, and the faithful performance of his ministerial office. He shall have his name recorded on the journal of said Convention, and also enrolled on a class paper, and shall meet in class; and in neglect of the above duties, the Quarterly Convention, if they judge it proper, may deprive him of his ministerial office. And when a preacher is located, or discontinued by an Annual Convention, he shall be amenable to the Quarterly Convention of the circuit or station where he had his last appointment, or at the place where he shall reside at the time of his location.

5. Let the appointments be so arranged as to give the local preachers regular and systematic employment on the Sabbath.

SECTION XVIII.

OFFICIAL MEETINGS.

1. An official meeting, composed of the preachers, exhorters, stewards, class leaders and Sunday school superintendents, shall be held in each circuit or station once a month wherever practicable.

2. The official board shall look after the temporal and spiritual interests of the circuit or station, establish and maintain Sunday schools, grant and renew licenses to exhort, provided that no person shall be licensed to exhort without a recommendation from the society* of which he is a member. They shall also recommend suitable persons to the Quarterly Convention to be licensed as local preachers.

3. The preacher in charge shall be chairman of the official meeting, and in his absence a chairman shall be elected. A secretary shall be elected once a year, who shall keep and record in a suitable book provided for the purpose, faithful minutes of the proceedings of the official meetings, and also of the meetings of the society. He shall also keep a record of all the money raised on the circuit for religious purposes, and of the manner in which the same was expended.

---

* By a "Society" is meant all the members of our Church, who meet together statedly, in one place, for public worship.

CHAPTER IV.

OF THE MEANS OF GRACE.

SECTION I.

Of Public Worship.

Quest. 1. What directions shall be given for the establishment of uniformity in public worship among us, on the Lord's day?

Answ. 1. Let the morning's service consist of singing, prayer, the reading of a chapter out of the Old Testament, and another out of the New, and preaching.

2. Let the afternoon service consist of singing, prayer, the reading of one or two chapters out of the Bible, and preaching.

3. Let the evening service consist of singing, prayer and preaching.

4. But on the days of administering the Lord's supper, the two chapters in the morning sevice may be omitted.

5. In administering the ordinances, and in the burial of the dead, let the form of Discipline invariably be used. Let the Lord's prayer also be used on all occasions of public worship in concluding the first prayer, and the apostolic benediction in dismissing the congregation.

6. Let the society be met, wherever it is practicable, on the Sabbath-day.

Quest. 2. Is there not a great indecency

sometimes practised among us, namely, talking in the congregation before and after services. How shall this be cured?

Answ. Let all the ministers and preachers join as one man, and enlarge on the impropriety of talking before or after service; and strongly exhort those that are concerned to do it no more. In three months, if we are in earnest, this vile practice will be banished out of every Methodist congregation. Let none stop till he he has carried his point.

SECTION II.

Of the Spirit and truth of Singing.

Quest. How shall we guard against formality in singing?

Answ. 1. Choose such hymns as are proper for the occasion, and do not sing too much at once. Seldom more than four or five verses.

2. Let the tune be suited to the sentiment, and do not suffer the people to sing too slow.

3. In every society let due attention be given to the cultivation of sacred music.

4. If you cannot sing yourself, let one or two be chosen in each society to lead the singing.

5. As singing is a part of Divine worship in which all ought to unite, therefore exhort every person in the congregation to sing, not one in ten only.

6. In no case let there be instrumental music or choir singing in our public worship.

SECTION III.

Of Class-meetings.

1. Let no person not a member of our Church, be admitted to a class meeting, without the consent of the Leader.

2. Let each Leader carefully inquire how every soul of his class prospers: not only how each person observes the outward rules, but how he grows in the knowledge and love of God.

3. Let the Leaders converse with those who have the charge of their circuits.

4. Let improper Leaders be changed.

5. Let the Leaders frequently meet each other's classes.

6. Let us observe which Leaders are the most useful; and let these meet the other classes as often as possible.

7. See that all the Leaders be not only men of sound judgment, but men truly devoted to God.

Quest. What shall we do with those members of our Church who wilfully and repeatedly neglect to meet their class?

Answ. 1. Let the Elder, Deacon, or one of the preachers visit them, whenever it is practicable, and explain to them the consequence if they continue to neglect, namely, exclusion.

2. If they do not amend, let them be brought to trial for neglect of duty.

SECTION IV.

Of Love Feasts.

1. Let a Love-feast be held on each circuit or station, at least once in three months.

2. Let no person not a member of our Church, be admitted to our Love-feasts without the consent of the preacher having charge of the same.

3. Let our Love-feasts be held with closed doors.

CHAPTER V.

OF DRESS AND MARRIAGE.

SECTION I.

Of Dress.

Quest. Should we insist on the rules concerning dress?

Answ. By all means. This is no time to give encouragement to superfluity of apparel. Therefore, receive none into the Church till they have left off all superfluous ornaments. In order to this: 1. Let every one who has charge of a circuit or station, read Mr. Wesley's

Thoughts upon Dress, at least once a year in every society. 2. In visiting the classes be very mild, but very strict. 3. Allow of no exempt case; better one suffer than many.

SECTION II.

Of Marriage.

Quest. 1. Do we observe any evil which has prevailed in our Church with respect to marriage?

Answ. Many of our members have married with *unawakened* persons. This has produced bad effects; they have been either hindered for life, or have turned back to perdition.

Qvest. 2. What can be done to discourage this?

Answ. 1. Let every preacher publicly enforce the apostle's caution, "Be ye not unequally yoked together with unbelievers." 2 Cor. vi, 4.

2. Let all be exhorted to take no step in so weighty a matter, without advising with the most serious of their brethren.

Quest. 3. Ought any woman to marry without the consent of her parents?

Answ. In general she ought not. Yet there may be exceptions. For if, 1. A woman believe it to be her duty to marry: if, 2. Her parents absolutely refuse to let her marry any Christian: then she may, nay, ought to marry without their consent. Yet even then a Methodist preacher ought not to be married to her.

We do not prohibit our people from marrying persons who are not of our Church, provided such persons have the form, and are seeking the power of godliness; but we are determined to discourage their marrying persons who do not come up to this description.

CHAPTER VI.

OF CHURCH TRIALS.

SECTION I.

Of the Trial of Ministers and Members.

1. Every crime forbidden in the word of God sufficient to exclude a person from the kingdom of grace and glory, shall subject a minister or member to expulsion from the Church.

2. The neglect of duties required by the word of God, or the indulgence in sinful tempers, words or actions, shall subject the person so offending to private reproof by the official member of the Church, having the oversight of the offending brother; and in case of persistence after proper admonition and labor, to trial and expulsion.

3. Any preacher or member against whom a charge is brought, shall be furnished by the person bringing the charge, or by the presiding officer of the tribunal to which he is judicially responsible, with a copy of the charges against

him, at least fourteen days before the trial, unless all the parties shall agree upon an earlier time for the trial.

4. An accused party shall be entitled to the assistance of such counsel as he may select from the members or ministers of our Church.

5. When charges are preferred against a member, the preacher shall call a meeting of the society who shall select a committee of not less than three, nor more than nine, to try the case. Both the accused and accuser shall have the right of challenge for cause, the validity of which shall be determined by the society. If the accused be a female she shall be tried before a committee of females if she so desires. The preacher in charge shall preside at the trial of members; but the chairman of the district may, for sufficient reasons, appoint some other preacher of the district to preside at any particular trial.

Any member who has been tried and convicted by a committee shall be entitled to an appeal to the next Quarterly Convention, provided he did not voluntarily absent himself from the trial, and provided he gave notice of his intention to appeal at the time of his condemnation or as soon thereafter as he was notified thereof.

6. An accused local preacher shall be tried by the Quarterly Convention of which he is a member, or by a committee of not less than three, nor more than nine, local preachers, called

by the chairman of the district, who shall preside at the trial. Any local preacher feeling aggrieved at the decision of his case shall be allowed an appeal to the ensuing session of the Annual Convention.

7. If a charge of immorality is brought against a traveling preacher in the intervals of the Annual Convention, the chairman of the district shall call a committee of not less than three, nor more than six, traveling preachers, and an equal number of laymen who were members of the last Annual Convention, who shall have power to suspend until the next session of the Annual Convention, with whom shall rest the decision of the case.

8. Each Annual Convention shall have original jurisdiction over all the preachers belonging thereto, and shall have power to reprove, suspend, locate for inefficiency or want of usefulness, or expel, according to the nature of the case, and as righteousness may require, All cases brought before an Annual Convention, either by complaint or by appeal, may be referred to a committee of six from each branch, who in the presence of the President of the Convention, either during its session or after its adjournment, shall try the case and decide it upon its merits; and their decision shall have the same effect as that of the Annual Convention.

9. The General Convention at each session,

shall appoint a standing committee on appeals, composed of four ministers, and four members from each of the Annual Conventions, who shall, if necessary, hold a session once a year, for the purpose of trying all appeals that may be taken by any traveling preachers from the decision of an Annual Convention. The President of the General Convention, or one of the superintendents, shall preside at the trial of appeal cases. Nine members of the committee on appeals shall constitute a quorum.

10. In all trials the proceedings shall be taken down by a Secretary appointed by the court; and when an appeal is taken, the case shall be decided from the testimony as it appears upon the record.

11. After such forms of trial and expulsion such person shall have no privileges of society or of sacraments in our Church without contrition, confession, and satisfactory reformation.

SECTION II.

Of Insolvencies, and the settlement of Disputes.

Quest. 1. How shall disputes between members of our Church, concerning the payment of debts or otherwise be settled?

Answ. 1. On any dispute between two or more of the members of our Church, concerning the payment of debts, or otherwise, which cannot be settled by the parties concerned, the preacher who has the charge of the circuit shall inquire into the circumstances of the case; and shall recommend to the contending parties a reference, consisting of one arbiter chosen by the plaintiff, and another chosen by the defendant; which two arbiters so chosen shall nominate the third; the three arbiters being members of our Church.

But if one of these parties be dissatisfied with the judgment given, such party may apply to the ensuing Quarterly Convention for allowance to have a *second* arbitration appointed; and if the Quarterly Convention see sufficient reason, they shall grant a *second* arbitration, in which case each party shall choose two arbiters, and the four arbiters shall choose a fifth, the judgment of the majority of whom shall be final; and any person refusing to abide by such judgment shall be excluded the Church.

And if any member of our Church shall refuse, in case of debt or other disputes, to refer the matter to arbitration, when recommended by him who has the charge of the circuit, or shall enter into a lawsuit with another member before these measures are taken, he shall be expelled, unless the case be of such a nature as to require or justify a process at law.

2. Whenever a complaint is made against any member of Church for non-payment of debt; when the accounts are adjusted, and the amount ascertained, the preacher having the charge shall

call the debtor before a committee of at least three, to show cause why he does not make payment. The committee shall determine what further time shall be granted him for payment, and what security shall be given for payment; and in case the debtor refuses to comply he shall be expelled; but in such case he may appeal to the Quarterly Convention, and their decision shall be final. And in case the creditor complains that justice is not done him, he may lay his grievance before the Quarterly Convention, and their decision shall be final; and if the creditor refuse to comply he shall be expelled.

Quest. 2. What shall be done in case of insolvency on the part of any of our members?

Answ. 1. The preachers who have the oversight of circuits are required to execute all our rules fully and strenuously against all frauds, and particularly against dishonest insolvencies: suffering none to remain in our Church on any account who are found guilty of any fraud.

2. To prevent scandal, when any of our members fail in business, or contract debts which they are not able to pay, let two or three judicious members of the Church inspect the accounts, contracts, and circumstances of the case of the supposed delinquent; and if he has behaved dishonestly, or borrowed money without a probability of paying, let him be expelled.

CHAPTER VII.

SECTION I.

Of Baptism.

1.   Let every adult person, and the parents of every child to be baptized, have the choice either of immersion, sprinkling, or pouring.

2.   We will on no account whatever make a charge for administering baptism, or for burying the dead.

SECTION II.

The Ministration of Baptism to Infants.

The minister coming to the font, which is to be filled with pure water, shall use the following:

Dearly beloved, forasmuch as our Saviour Christ saith, None can enter into the kingdom of God, except he be regenerate and born anew of water and of the Holy Ghost; I beseech you to call upon God the Father, through our Lord Jesus Christ, that of his bounteous mercy he will grant to *this child* that thing which by nature *he* cannot have, that *he* may be baptized with water and the Holy Ghost, and received into Christ's holy Church, and be made a *lively member* of the same.

5

Then shall the minister say,
Let us pray.

Almighty and everlasting God, we beseech thee, for thine infinite mercies, that thou wilt look upon *this child:* wash *him* and sanctify *him* with the Holy Ghost; that *he,* being delivered from thy wrath, may be received into the ark of Christ's Church, and being steadfast in faith, joyful through hope, and rooted in love, may so pass the waves of this troublesome world, that finally *he* may come to the land of everlasting life; there to reign with thee, world without end, through Jesus Christ our Lord. *Amen.*

O merciful God, grant that the old Adam in *this child* may be so buried, that the new man may be raised up in *him.*   *Amen.*

Grant that all carnal affections may die in *him,* and that all things belonging to the Spirit may live and grow in *him.*   *Amen.*

Grant that *he* may have power and strength to have victory, and to triumph against the devil, the world, and the flesh.   *Amen.*

Grant that whosoever is dedicated to thee by our office and ministry may also be endued with heavenly virtues, and everlastingly rewarded through thy mercy, O blessed Lord God, who dost live and govern all things, world without end.   *Amen.*

Almighty, ever-living God, whose most dearly-beloved Son Jesus Christ, died for the forgiveness of our sins, and gave commandment to his disciples that they should go teach all nations, and baptize them in the name of the Father, and of the Son, and of the Holy Ghost, regard, we beseech thee, the supplications of thy congregation; sanctify this water for this holy sacrament; and grant that *this child* now to be baptized may receive the fullness of thy grace, and ever remain in the number of thy faithful and elect children, through Jesus Christ our Lord. *Amen.*

*Then shall the people stand up; and the minister
shall say,*

Hear the words of the Gospel written by St. Mark in the tenth chapter, at the thirteenth verse.

They brought young children to Christ, that he should touch them. And his disciples rebuked those that brought them; but when Jesus saw it, he was much displeased, and said unto them, Suffer little children to come unto me, and forbid them not, for 'of such is the kingdom of God. Verily I say unto you, Whosoever shall not receive the kingdom of God as a little child, he shall not enter therein. And he took them up in his arms, put his hands upon them, and blessed them.

*Then the minister shall take the child into his hands,
and say to the friends of the child,*

Name this child.

And then naming it after them, he shall sprinkle or pour water upon it, or, if desired, immerse it in water, saying,

N. I baptize thee in the name of the Father, and of the Son, and of the Holy Ghost. *Amen.*

Then shall be said, all kneeling,

Our Father who art in heaven, hallowed be thy name; thy kingdom come; thy will be done, on earth as it is in heaven: give us this day our daily bread, and forgive us our trespasses, as we forgive them that trespass against us; and lead us not into temptation, but deliver us from evil. *Amen.*

Then shall the minister conclude with extemporary prayer.

SECTION III.

The Ministration of Baptism to such as are of Riper Years.

Dearly Beloved, Since all men are by nature sinners, and have nothing in themselves by which they can be delivered from the guilt and pollution of sin, and attain to that holiness without which no man can see the Lord, we invite you to join with us in fervent prayer for these persons, that they may have grace always to keep their covenant with God, and that they may continually enjoy the washing of regeneration, and the renewing of the Holy Ghost.

Then shall the minister say.

Almighty and Immortal God, the aid of all that need, the helper of all that flee to thee for succor, the life of them that believe, and the resurrection of the dead: we call upon thee for *these persons;* that *they,* coming to thy holy baptism, may receive the inward baptism of the Holy Ghost. Receive *them,* O Lord, as thou hast promised by thy well-beloved Son, saying, Ask, and ye shall receive; seek, and ye shall find; knock, and it shall be opened unto you: so give now unto us that ask: let us that seek, find : open the gate unto us that knock; that *these persons* may enjoy the everlasting benediction of thy heavenly washing, and may come to the eternal kingdom which thou hast promised by Christ our Lord. *Amen.*

Then shall the people stand up, and the minister shall say,

Hear the words of the Gospel written by St. John, in the third chapter.

Verily, verily, I say unto thee, Except a man be born of water, and of the Spirit, he cannot enter into the kingdom of God. That which is born of the flesh is flesh; and that which is born of the Spirit is spirit. Marvel not that I said unto thee, Ye must be born again. The wind bloweth where it listeth, and thou hearest the sound thereof, but thou canst not tell whence it

cometh, and whither it goeth: so is every one
that is born of the Spirit.

*Then the minister shall speak to the persons to be
baptized on this wise.*

Well beloved, who *are* come hither, desiring
to receive holy baptism, *ye* have heard how the
congregation hath prayed that our Lord Jesus
Christ would vouchsafe to receive you, and bless
you, to release you of your sins, to give you the
kingdom of heaven, and everlasting life. And
our Lord Jesus Christ hath promised, in his holy
word, to grant all those things that we have
prayed for: which promise he for his part will
most surely keep and perform.

Wherefore after this promise made by Christ,
you must also faithfully, for *your* part, promise,
in the presence of this whole congregation, that
you will renounce the devil and all his works,
and constantly believe God's holy word, and obediently keep his commandments.

*Then shall the minister demand of each of the persons
to be baptized, severally,*

Quest. Dost thou renounce the devil and all
his works, the vain pomp and glory of the
world, with all covetous desires of the same, and
the carnal desires of the flesh, so that thou wilt
not follow or be led by them?

Answ. I renounce them all.

Quest. Dost thou believe in God the Father

Almighty, Maker of heaven and earth? and in
Jesus Christ his only begotten Son our Lord?
and that he was conceived by the Holy Ghost,
born of the Virgin Mary? that he suffered under
Pontius Pilate, was crucified, dead and buried:
that he rose again the third day; that he ascended into heaven, and sitteth at the right hand
of God the Father Almighty, and from thence
shall come again, at the end of the world, to
judge the quick and the dead?

And dost thou believe in the Holy Ghost, the
communion of saints; the remission of sins; the
resurrection of the body, and everlasting life after death?

Answ. All this I steadfastly believe.

Quest. Wilt thou be baptized in this faith?

Answ. This is my desire.

Quest. Wilt thou then obediently keep God's
holy will and commandments, and walk in the
same all the days of thy life?

Answ. I will endeavor so to do, God being my
helper.

Then shall the minister say,

O merciful God, grant that the old Adam *in
these persons* may be so buried, that the new
man may be raised up in *them. Amen.*

Grant that all carnal affections may die in
them, and that all things belonging to the Spirit
may live and grow in *them. Amen.*

Grant that *they* may have power and strength

to have victory, and triumph against the devil, the world, and the flesh. *Amen.*

Grant that *they* being here dedicated to thee by our office and ministry, may also be endued with heavenly virtues, and everlastingly rewarded, through thy mercy, O blessed Lord God, who dost live and govern all things, world without end. *Amen.*

Almighty, ever-living God, whose most dearly-beloved Son Jesus Christ, died for the forgiveness of our sins; and gave commandment to his disciples that they should go teach all nations, and baptize them in the name of the Father, and of the Son, and of the Holy Ghost: regard, we beseech thee, the supplications of this congregation; and grant that the *persons* now to be baptized may receive the fullness of thy grace, and ever remain in the number of thy faithful and elect children, through Jesus Christ our Lord. *Amen.*

Then shall the minister take each person to be baptized by the right hand: and placing him conveniently by the font, according to his discretion, shall ask the name; and then shall sprinkle or pour water upon him, (or if he shall desire it, shall immerse him in water,) saying,

N. I baptize thee in the name of the Father, and of the Son, and of the Holy Ghost. *Amen.*

Then shall be said the Lord's Prayer, all kneeling. Concluding with extemporary prayer, and the benediction.

CHAPTER VIII.

THE LORD'S SUPPER.

SECTION I.

General Directions.

1. No person shall be admitted to the Lord's Supper among us who is guilty of any immoral or unchristian practice for which we would exclude a member of our Church.

2. All persons properly included in the general invitation may be allowed to partake of the Lord's Supper among us.

SECTION II.

The Order for the Administration of the Lord's Supper.

The elder shall say one or more of these sentences :

Let your light so shine before men, that they may see your good works, and glorify your Father which is in heaven. Matt. v, 16.

Lay not up for yourselves treasures upon earth, where moth and rust doth corrupt, and where thieves break through and steal: but lay up for yourselves treasures in heaven, where neither moth nor rust doth corrupt, and where thieves do not break through nor steal. Matt. vi, 19, 20.

Whatsoever ye would that men should do to

you, do ye even so to them: for this is the law
and the prophets.   Matt. vii, 12.

Not every one that saith unto me, Lord, Lord,
shall enter into the kindgdom of heaven; but
he that doeth the will of my Father which is in
heaven.   Matt. vii, 21.

Zaccheus stood, and said unto the Lord, Behold, Lord, the half of my goods I give to the
poor; and if I have taken anything from any
man, by false accusation, I restore him fourfold.
Luke xix, 8.

He which soweth sparingly shall reap also
sparingly; and he which soweth bountifully shall
reap also bountifully.   Every man according as
he purposeth in his heart, so let him give ; not
grudgingly, or of necessity; for God loveth a
cheerful giver.   2 Cor. ix, 6, 7.

As we have therefore opportunity, let us do
good unto all men, especially unto them who are
of the household of faith.   Gal. vi, 10.

Godliness with contentment is great gain; for
we brought nothing into this world, and it is
certain we can carry nothing out. 1 Tim. vi, 6, 7.

Charge them that are rich in this world, that
they be ready to distribute, willing to communicate, laying up in store for themselves a good
foundation against the time to come, that they
may lay hold on eternal life.   1 Tim. vi, 17, 19.

God is not unrighteous to forget your work
and labor of love, which ye have showed toward
his name, in that ye have ministered to the
saints, and do minister.   Heb. vi, 10.

To do good, and to communicate, forget not; for with such sacrifices God is well pleased. Heb. xiii, 16.

Whoso hath this world's good, and seeth his brother have need, and shutteth up his bowels of compassion from him, how dwelleth the love of God in him? 1 John iii, 17.

He that hath pity upon the poor, lendeth unto the Lord; and that which he hath given will he pay him again. Prov. xix, 17.

Blessed is he that considereth the poor; the Lord will deliver him in time of trouble. Psalm xli, 1.

While these sentences are being read, let a collection be taken up.

After which the elder shall say,

Ye that do truly and earnestly repent of your sins, and are in love and charity with your neighbors, and intend to lead a new life, following the commandments of God, and walking from henceforth in his holy ways; draw near with faith, and take this holy sacrament to your comfort: and make your humble confession to Almighty God, meekly kneeling upon your knees.

Then shall this general confession be made by the minister in the name of all those who are minded to receive the holy communion, both he and all the people kneeling humbly upon their knees, and saying,

Almighty God, Father of our Lord Jesus

Christ, Maker of all things, Judge of all men:
we acknowledge and bewail our manifold sins
and wickedness, which we from time to time
most grieviously have committed, by thought,
word, and deed, against thy Divine Majesty,
provoking most justly thy wrath and indignation
against us. We do earnestly repent, and are
heartily sorry for these our misdoings; the remembrance of them is grievous unto us. Have
mercy upon us, have mercy upon us, most merciful
Father; for thy Son, our Lord Jesus Christ's
sake, forgive us all that is past; and grant that
we may ever hereafter serve and please thee in
newness of life, to the honor and glory of thy
name, through Jesus Christ our Lord. *Amen.*

Then shall the elder say,

O Almighty God, our heavenly Father, who
of thy great mercy hast promised forgiveness of
sins to all them that with hearty repentance and
true faith turn unto thee: have mercy upon us;
pardon and deliver us from our sins, confirm and
strengthen us in all goodness, and bring us to
everlasting life, through Jesus Christ our Lord.
Amen.

The collect.

Almighty God, unto whom all hearts be open,
all desires known, and from whom no secrets are
hid; cleanse the thoughts of our hearts by the
inspiration of thy Holy Spirit, that we may per-

fectly love thee, and worthily magnify thy holy
name, through Christ our Lord.   *Amen.*

Then shall the elder say,

It is very meet, right, and our bounden duty,
that we should at all times, and in all places,
give thanks unto thee, O Lord, holy Father, almighty and everlasting God.

Therefore with angels and archangels, and
with all the company of heaven, we laud and
magnify thy glorious name, evermore praising
thee, and saying, Holy, holy, holy, Lord God of
hosts, heaven and earth are full of thy glory.
Glory be to thee, O Lord most high.   *Amen.*

Then shall the elder say,

We do not presume to come to this thy table,
O merciful Lord, trusting in our own righteousness, but in thy manifold and great mercies. We
are not worthy so much as to gather up the
crumbs under thy table. But thou art the same
Lord, whose property is always to have mercy:
Grant us, therefore, gracious Lord, so to eat
the flesh of thy dear Son Jesus Christ, and to
drink his blood, that our sinful souls and bodies
may be made clean by his death, and washed
through his most precious blood, and that we
may evermore dwell in him, and he in us. *Amen.*

*Then the elder shall say the prayer of consecration,
as follows:*

Almighty God, our heavenly Father, who of

thy tender mercy didst give thine only Son Jesus Christ to suffer death upon the cross for our redemption; who made there (by his oblation of himself once offered) a full, perfect, and sufficient sacrifice, oblation, and satisfaction, for the sins of the whole world; and did institute, and in his holy gospel command us to continue, a perpetual memory of that his precious death until his coming again: hear us, O merciful Father, we most humbly beseech thee, and grant that we, receiving these thy creatures of bread and wine, according to thy Son our Saviour Jesus Christ's holy institution, in remembrance of his death and passion, may be partakers of his most blessed body and blood; who in the same night that he was betrayed, took bread; (1) and when he had given thanks, he broke it (2) and gave it to his disciples, saying, Take, eat; this (3) is my body which is given for you; do this in remembrance of me. Likewise after supper he took (4) the cup; and when he had given thanks, he gave it to them, saying, Drink ye all of this: for this (5) is my blood of the New Testament, which is shed for you and for many, for

(1) *Here the elder is to take the plate of bread into his hand.*

(2) *And here to break the bread.*

(3) *And here to lay his hands upon all the bread.*

(4) *Here he is to take the cup in his hand.*

(5) *And here to lay his hand upon all the vessels which contain the wine.*

the remission of sins; do this, as oft as ye shall drink it, in remembrance of me. *Amen.*

Then shall the minister first receive the communion in both kinds himself, and then proceed to deliver the same to the other ministers in like manner, (if any there be present,) and after that to the people also, in order, into their hands. And when he delivereth the bread, he shall say,

The body of our Lord Jesus Christ, which was given for *thee*, preserve *thy soul* and *body* unto everlasting life. Take and eat this in re-membrance that Christ died for *thee*, and feed on him in *thy heart* by faith with thanksgiving.

And the minister that delivereth the cup shall say,

The blood of our Lord Jesus Christ, which was shed for *thee*, preserve *thy soul* and *body* un-to everlasting life. Drink this in remembrance that Christ's blood was shed for *thee*, and be thankful.

[If the consecrated bread or wine shall be all spent before all have commuicated, the elder may consecrate more, by repeating the prayer of consecration,]

[When all have communicated, the minister shall return to the Lord's table, and place upon it what re-maineth of the consecrated elements, covering the same with a fair linen cloth.]

Then shall the elder say the Lord's Prayer; the peo-ple repeating after him every petition.

Our Father who art in heaven, hallowed be

thy name: thy kingdom come: thy will be done on earth as it is in heaven : give us this day our daily bread; and forgive us our trespasses, as we forgive them that trespass against us: and lead us not into temptation, but deliver us from evil, for thine is the kingdom, and the power, and the glory, for ever and ever. *Amen.*

Concluding with this blessing:—

May the peace of God, which passeth all understanding, keep your hearts and minds in the knowledge and love of God, and of his Son Jesus Christ our Lord; and the blessings of God Almighty, the Father, the Son, and the Holy Ghost, be among you and remain with you always. *Amen.*

N. B.—If the elder be straitened for time, he may omit any part of the service except the prayer of consecration.

CHAPTER IX.

FORMS OF ORDINATION.

SECTION I.

The Form and Manner of ordaining Elders.

[When the day appointed for the ordination is come, there shall be a sermon or exhortation, declaring the duty and office of such as come to be admitted elders; how necessary that order is in the Church of Christ, and also how the people ought to esteem them in their office.]

After which, one of the elders shall present unto the president all them that are to be ordained, and say,

I present unto you these persons present to be ordained elders.

Then their names being read aloud, the president shall say unto the people,

Brethren, these are they whom we purpose, God willing, this day to ordain elders.   For after due examination, we find not to the contrary, but that they are lawfully called to this function and ministry, and that they are persons meet for the same.   But if there be any of you who knoweth any impediment or crime in any of them, for the which he ought not to be received into this holy ministry, let him come forth in the name of God, and show what the crime or impediment is.

[If any crime or impediment be objected, the president shall surcease from ordaining that person until such time as the party accused shall be found clear of the crime.]

Then shall be said the collect, epistle, and gospel as followeth:

The Collect.

Almighty God, Giver of all good things, who by thy Holy Spirit hast appointed divers orders of ministers in thy Church; mercifully behold these thy servants now called to the office of

elders, and replenish them so with the truth of
thy doctrine, and adorn them with innocency
of life, that both by word and good example
they may faithfully serve thee in this office, to
the glory of thy name, and the edification of
thy Church, through the mercies of our Saviour
Jesus Christ, who liveth and reigneth with thee
and the Holy Ghost, world without end. *Amen.*

The Epistle. Eph. iv, 7-13.

Unto every one of us is given grace according to the measure of the gift of Christ. Wherefore he saith, when he ascended up on high, he
led captivity captive, and gave gifts unto men.
(Now that he ascended, what is it but that he
also descended first into the lower parts of the
earth? He that descended is the same also
that ascended up far above all heavens, that he
might fill all things.) And he gave some,
apostles; and some, prophets; and some, evangelists; and some pastors and teachers; for the
perfecting of the saints, for the work of the
ministry, for the edifying of the body of Christ,
till we all come in the unity of faith, and of the
knowledge of the Son of God, unto a perfect
man, unto the measure of the stature of the
fullness of Christ.

*After this shall be read for the Gospel, part of the
tenth chapter of St. John.*

St. John x, 1-16.

Verily, verily, I say unto you, He that enter-

eth not by the door into the sheepfold, but
climbeth up some other way, the same is a thief
and a robber. But he that entereth in by the
door is the shepherd of the sheep. To him the
porter openeth, and the sheep hear his voice,
and he calleth his own sheep by name, and
leadeth them out. And when he putteth forth
his own sheep, he goeth before them, and the
sheep follow him, for they know his voice. And
a stranger will they not follow, but will flee
from him, for they know not the voice of stran-
gers. This parable spake Jesus unto them, but
they understood not what things they were
which he spake unto them. Then said Jesus
unto them again, Verily, verily, I say unto you,
I am the door of the sheep. All that ever
came before me are thieves and robbers, but the
sheep did not hear them. I am the door; by
me if any man enter in, he shall be saved, and
shall go in and out and find pasture. The
thief cometh not but for to steal, and to kill,
and to destroy; I am come that they might
have life, and that they might have it more
abundantly. I am the good shepherd: the
good shepherd giveth his life for the sheep.
But he that is a hireling, and not the shepherd,
whose own the sheep are not, seeth the wolf
coming, and leaveth the sheep, and fleeth, and
the wolf catcheth them, and scattereth the
sheep. The hireling fleeth because he is a
hireling, and careth not for the sheep. I am

the good shepherd, and know my sheep, and
am known of mine. As the Father knoweth
me, even so know I the Father: and I lay
down my life for the sheep. And other sheep I
have which are not of this fold: them also I
must bring, and they shall hear my voice, and
there shall be one fold and one shepherd.

*And that done, the president shall say unto them as
hereafter followeth :*

You have heard, brethren, as well in your
private examination as in the exhortation
which was now made to you, and in the holy
lessons taken out of the Gospel, and the wri-
tings of the apostles, of what dignity, and of
how great importance this office is whereunto
ye are called. And now again we exhort you in
the name of our Lord Jesus Christ, that you have
in remembrance, into how high a dignity and
to how weighty an office ye are called; that is
to say, to be messengers, watchmen, and stewards of the Lord, to teach and to premonish, to
feed and provide for the Lord's family, to seek
for Christ's sheep that are dispersed abroad, and
for his children who are in the midst of this
evil world, that they may be saved through
Christ for ever.

Have always, therefore, printed in your remembrance how great a treasure is committed
to your charge. For they are the sheep of
Christ, which he bought with his death, and for

whom he shed his blood. The Church and congregation whom you must serve, is his spouse and his body. And if it shall happen, the same Church, or any member thereof, do take any hurt or hinderance by reason of your negligence, ye know the greatness of the fault, and also the horrible punishment that will ensue. Wherefore consider with yourselves the end of the ministry toward the children of God, toward the spouse and body of Christ; and see that you never cease your labor, your care and diligence, until you have done all that lieth in you, according to your bounden duty, to bring all such as are or shall be committed to your charge, unto that agreement in the faith and knowledge of God, and to that ripeness and perfectness of age in Christ, that there be no place left among you, either for error in religion, or for viciousness in life.

Forasmuch then, as your office is both of so great excellency, and of so great difficulty, ye see with how great care and study ye ought to apply yourselves, as well that ye may show yourselves dutiful and thankful unto that Lord who hath placed you in so high a dignity; as also to beware that neither you yourselves offend, nor be occasion that others offend. Howbeit ye cannot have a mind and will thereto of yourselves; for that will and ability is given of God alone: therefore ye ought, and have need to pray earnestly for his Holy Spirit. And see,

ing that ye cannot by any other means compass
the doing of so weighty a work, pertaining to
the salvation of man, but with doctrine and exhortation taken out of the Holy Scriptures, and
with a life agreeable to the same; consider how
studious ye ought to be in reading and learning
the Scriptures, and in framing the manners,
both of yourselves and of them that specially
pertain unto you, according to the rule of the
same Scriptures: and for this self-same cause,
how ye ought to forsake and set aside (as much
as you may) all worldly cares and studies.

We have good hope that you have all weighed
and pondered these things with yourselves long
before this time: and that you have clearly determined, by God's grace, to give yourselves
wholly to this office, whereunto it hath pleased
God to call you; so that as much as lieth in you,
you will apply yourselves wholly to this one
thing, and draw all your cares and studies this
way, and that you will continually pray to God
the Father, by the mediation of our only Saviour
Jesus Christ, for the heavenly assistance of the
Holy Ghost; that by daily reading and weigh-
ing of the Scriptures, ye may wax riper and
stronger in your ministry; and that ye may so
endeavor yourselves from time to time to sanctify the lives of you and yours, and to fashion
them after the rule and doctrine of Christ, that
ye may be wholesome and godly examples and
patterns for the people to follow.

And now that this present congregation of Christ, here assembled, may also understand your minds and wills in these things, and that this your promise may the more move you to do your duties: ye shall answer plainly to these things which we, in the name of God and his Church, shall demand of you touching the same.

Do you think in your heart that you are truly called, according to the will of our Lord Jesus Christ, to the order of elders?

Answ. I think so.

The president. Are you persuaded that the Holy Scriptures contain sufficiently all doctrine required of necessity for eternal salvation through faith in Jesus Christ? And are you determined out of the said Scriptures to instruct the people committed to your charge, and to teach nothing as required of necessity to eternal salvation, but that which you shall be persuaded may be concluded and proved by the Scripture?

Answ. I am so persuaded, and have so determined, by God's grace.

The president. Will you then give your faithful diligence always so to minister the doctrines and sacraments, and discipline of Christ, as the Lord hath commanded?

Answ. I will so do, by the help of the Lord.

The President. Will you be ready with all faithful diligence to banish and drive away all erroneous and strange doctrines contrary to God's

word; and to use both public and private moni-
tions and exhortations, as well to the sick as to
the whole within your charge, as need shall require and occasion shall be given?

Answ. I will, the Lord being my helper.

The president. Will you be diligent in prayers,
and in reading of the Holy Scriptures, and in
such studies as help to the knowledge of the
same, laying aside the study of the world and
the flesh?

Answ. I will endeavor so to do, the Lord being my helper.

The president. Will you be diligent to frame
and fashion yourselves, and your families, according to the doctrine of Christ; and to make
both yourselves and them, as much as in you
lieth, wholesome examples and patterns to the
flock of Christ?

Answ. I shall apply myself thereto, the Lord
being my helper.

The president. Will you maintain and set forward, as much as lieth in you, quietness, peace,
and love, among all Christian people, and especially among them that are or shall be committed to your charge?

Answ. I will do so, the Lord being my helper.

*That done, the president shall pray in this wise, and
say,*

Let us pray.

Almighty God and heavenly Father, who of
thine infinite love and goodness toward us, hast

given to us thy only and most dearly beloved Son Jesus Christ to be our Redeemer, and the author of everlasting life; who after he had made perfect our redemption by his death, and was ascended into heaven, sent abroad into the world his apostles, prophets, evangelists, doctors, and pastors, by whose labor and ministry he gathered together a great flock in all parts of the world, to set forth the eternal praise of thy holy name; for these so great benefits of thy eternal goodness, and for that thou hast vouchsafed to call these thy servants here present to the same office and ministry appointed for the salvation of mankind, we render unto thee most hearty thanks; we praise and worship thee; and we humbly beseech thee by the same, thy blessed Son, to grant unto all who either here or elsewhere call upon thy name, that we may continue to show ourselves thankful unto thee for these, and all other thy benefits, and that we may daily increase and go forward in the knowledge and faith of thee and thy Son, by the Holy Spirit. So that as well by these thy ministers, as by them over whom they shall be appointed thy ministers, thy holy name may be forever glorified, and thy blessed kingdom enlarged, through the same, thy Son Jesus Christ our Lord; who liveth and reigneth with thee in the unity of the same Holy Spirit, world without end. *Amen.*

*When this prayer is done, the president with the el-
ders present, shall lay their hands severally upon
the head of every one that receiveth the order of
elders; the receivers humbly kneeling upon their
knees, and the president saying,*

The Lord pour upon thee the Holy Ghost for
the office and work of an elder in the Church
of God, now committed unto thee by the imposi-
tion of our hands. And be thou a faithful dis-
penser of the word of God, and of his holy sacraments; in the name of the Father, and of
the Son, and of the Holy Ghost. *Amen.*

*Then the president shall deliver to every one of them,
kneeling, the Bible into his hands, saying,*

Take thou authority to preach the word of
God, and to administer the holy sacraments in
the congregation.

Then the president shall say,

Most merciful Father, we beseech thee to
send upon these thy servants thy heavenly blessings, that they may be clothed with righteousness, and that thy word spoken by their mouths
may have such success, that it may never be
spoken in vain. Grant also that we may have
grace to hear and receive what they shall deliver out of thy most holy word, or agreeably to
the same, as the means of our salvation; and
that in all our words and deeds we may seek
thy glory, and the increase of thy kingdom,
through Jesus Christ our Lord. *Amen.*

Assist us, O Lord, in all our doings, with thy most gracious favor, and further us with thy continual help, that in all our works begun, continued, and ended in thee, we may glorify thy holy name, and finally, by thy mercy obtain everlasting life, through Jesus Christ our Lord. *Amen.*

The peace of God which passeth all understanding, keep your hearts and minds in the knowledge and love of God, and of his Son Jesus Christ our Lord; and the blessing of God Almighty, the Father, the Son, and the Holy Ghost, be among you, and remain with you always. *Amen.*

SECTION II.

The Form and Manner of making of Deacons.

[When the day appointed for the ordination is come, there shall be a sermon or exhortation, declaring the duty and office of such as come to be admitted deacons.]

After which, one of the elders, shall present unto the president the persons to be ordained deacons, and their names being read aloud, the president shall say unto the people:

Brethren, if there be any of you who knoweth any impediment or crime in any of these persons presented to be ordained deacons, for the which he ought not to be admitted to that office, let him come forth in the name of

God, and show what the crime or impediment is.

[If any crime or impediment be objected, the president shall surcease from ordaining that person, until such time as the party accused shall be found clear of that crime.]

Then shall be read the following collect and epistle :

The Collect.

Almighty God, who by thy divine Providence hast appointed divers orders of ministers in thy Church, and who didst inspire thy apostles to choose into the order of deacons thy first martyr, St. Stephen, with others: mercifully behold these thy servants, now called to the like office and administration; replenish them so with the truth of thy doctrine, and adorn them with innocency of life, that both by word and good example they may faithfully serve thee in this office, to the glory of thy name, and the edification of thy Church, through the merits of our Saviour Jesus Christ, who liveth and reigneth with thee and the Holy Ghost now and forever. *Amen.*

The Epistle. 1 Tim. iii, 8–13.

Likewise must the deacons be grave, not doubled tongued, not given to much wine, not greedy of filthy lucre; holding the mystery of the faith in a pure conscience. And let these also first be proved; then let them use the office

of a deacon, being found blameless. Even so
must their wives be grave, not slanderers, sober,
faithful in all things. Let the deacons be the
husbands of one wife, ruling their children and
their own houses well. For they that have used
the office of a deacon well, purchase to themselves a good degree, and great boldness in the
faith which is in Christ Jesus.

*Then shall the president examine every one of those
who are to be ordained, in the presence of the people,
after this manner following :—*

Do you trust that you are inwardly moved by
the Holy Ghost to take upon you the office of
the ministry in the Church of Christ, to serve
God for the promoting of his glory and the edifying of his people?

Answ. I trust so.

The President. Do you unfeignedly believe all
the canonical Scriptures of the Old and New
Testament?

Answ. I do believe them.

The President. Will you diligently read or expound the same unto the people whom you shall
be appointed to serve?

Answ. I will.

The President. It appertaineth to the office of
a deacon to assist the elder in divine service.
And especially when he ministereth the holy
communion, to help him in the distribution
thereof, and to read and expound the Holy
Scriptures; to instruct the youth, and in the ab-

sence of the elder to baptize. And furthermore, it is his office to search for the sick, poor, and impotent, that they may be visited and relieved. Will you do this gladly and willingly?

Answ. I will do so by the help of God.

The President. Will you apply all your diligence to frame and fashion your own lives (and the lives of your families) according to the doctrine of Christ; and to make (both) yourselves (and them,) as much as in you lieth, wholesome examples of the flock of Christ?

Answ. I will do so, the Lord being my helper.

The President. Will you reverently obey them to whom the charge and government over you is committed, following with a glad mind and will their godly admonitions?

Answ. I will endeavor so to do, the Lord being my helper.

Then the President, laying his hands severally upon the head of every one of them, shall say,

Take thou authority to execute the office of a deacon in the Church of God; in the name of the Father, and of the Son, and of the Holy Ghost. *Amen.*

Then shall the president deliver to every one of them the Holy Bible, saying,

Take thou authority to read the Holy Scriptures in the Church of God, and to preach the same.

Then one of them appointed by the president shall read the Gospel.

Luke xii, 35–38.

Let your loins be girded about, and your lights burning, and ye yourselves like unto men that wait for their Lord, when he will return from the wedding, that when he cometh and knocketh, they may open unto him immediately. Blessed are those servants whom the Lord when he cometh shall find watching. Verily I say unto you, that he shall gird himself, and make them to sit down to meat, and will come forth and serve them. And if he shall come in the second watch, or come in the third watch, and find them so, blessed are those servants.

[Then shall the president proceed in the communion, and all that are ordained shall receive the holy communion.]

The communion ended, immediately before the benediction shall be said these collects following :—

Almighty God, Giver of all good things, who of thy great goodness hast vouchsafed to accept and take these thy servants into the office of deacons of thy Church ; make them, we beseech thee, O Lord, to be modest, humble, and constant in their ministration, and to have a ready will to observe all spiritual discipline ; that they having always the testimony of a good conscience, and continuing ever stable and strong in thy Son Christ Jesus, may so well behave themselves in this inferior office, that they may be found worthy to be called into the higher ministries in thy Church, through the same, thy Son our Saviour Jesus Christ; to whom be glory and honor, world without end. *Amen.*

Assist us, O Lord, in all our doings, with thy most gracious favor, and further us with thy continual help; that in all our works, begun, continued and ended in thee, we may glorify thy holy name, and finally, by thy mercy, obtain everlasting life, through Jesus Christ our Lord. *Amen.*

The peace of God, which passeth all understanding, keep your hearts and minds in the knowledge and love of God, and of his Son Jesus Christ our Lord. And the blessing of God Almighty, the Father, the Son, and the Holy Ghost, be among you, and remain with you always. *Amen.*

CHAPTER X.

THE FORM OF SOLEMNIZATION OF MATRIMONY.

At the day and time appointed for solemnization of matrimony, the persons to be married standing together, the man on the right hand, and the woman on the left, the minister shall say,

Dearly beloved, we are gathered together here in the sight of God, and in the presence of these witnesses, to join together this man and this woman in holy matrimony: which is an honorable estate, instituted of God in the time of man's innocency, signifying unto us the mystical union that is between Christ and his Church; which holy estate Christ adorned and beautified with his presence, and first miracle that he wrought in Cana of Galilee, and is commended of St. Paul to be honorable among all men; and therefore is not by any to be taken in hand unadvisedly, but reverently, discreetly, advisedly, and in the fear of God.

Into which holy estate these two persons present come now to be joined. Therefore, if any can show any just cause why they may not lawfully be joined together, let him now speak, or else hereafter for ever hold his peace.

And also speaking unto the persons that are to be married, he shall say.

I require and charge you both (as you will answer at the dreadful day of judgment, when the secrets of all hearts shall be disclosed) that if either of you know any impediment why you may not be lawfully joined together in matrimony, you do now confess it: for be ye well assured, that so many as are coupled together otherwise than God's word doth allow, are not joined together by God, neither is their matrimony lawful.

7

*If no impediment be alleged, then shall the minister
say unto the man,*

M., Wilt thou have this woman to thy wedded
wife, to live together after God's ordinance, in
the holy estate of matrimony? Wilt thou love
her, comfort her, honor, and keep her, in sickness
and in health: and, forsaking all other, keep
thee only unto her, so long as ye both shall live?

The man shall answer,

I will.

Then shall the minister say unto the woman,

N., Wilt thou have this man to thy wedded
husband, to live together after God's ordinance,
in the holy estate of matrimony? Wilt thou
obey him, serve him, love, honor, and keep him,
in sickness and in health: and, forsaking all
other, keep thee only unto him, so long as ye
both shall live?

The woman shall answer,

I will.

*Then the minister shall cause the man with his right
hand to take the woman by her right hand, and to
say after him as followeth:—*

I, *M.*, take thee, *N.*, to be my wedded wife, to
have and to hold, from this day forward, for better, for worse, for richer, for poorer, in sickness

and in health, to love and to cherish, till death do us part, according to God's holy ordinance: and thereunto I plight thee my faith.

Then shall they loose their hands, and the woman with her right hand taking the man by his right hand, shall likewise say after the minister:

I, *N.*, take thee, *M.*, to be my wedded husband, to have and to hold from this day forward, for better, for worse, for richer, for poorer, in sickness and in health, to love, cherish, and to obey, till death us do part, according to God's holy ordinance: and thereto I give thee my faith.

Then shall the minister join their right hands together, and say,

Those whom God hath joined together let no man put asunder.

Forasmuch as *M.* and *N.* have consented together in holy wedlock, and have witnessed the same before God and this company, and thereto have pledged their faith either to other, and have declared the same by joining of hands; I pronounce that they are man and wife together, in the name of the Father, and of the Son, and of the Holy Ghost. *Amen.*

And the minister shall add this blessing:—

God the Father, God the Son, God the Holy Ghost, bless, preserve, and keep you; the Lord mercifully with his favor look upon you, and so fill you with all spiritual benediction and grace, that ye may so live together in this life, that in the world to come ye may have life everlasting. *Amen.*

Then let prayer be offered.

CHAPTER XI.

ORDER OF THE BURIAL OF THE DEAD.

The minister, meeting the corpse, and going before it shall say,

I am the resurrection and the life: he that believeth in me, though he were dead, yet shall he live: and whosoever liveth and believeth in me, shall never die.   John **xi,** 25, 26.

I know that my Redeemer liveth, and that he shall stand at the latter day upon the earth; and though after my skin worms destroy this body, yet in my flesh shall I see God; whom I shall see for myself, and mine eyes shall behold, and not another.   Job xix, 25–27.

We brought nothing into this world, and it is certain we can carry nothing out. The Lord gave, and the Lord hath taken away; blessed be the name of the Lord.   1 Tim. vi, 7; Job i, 21.

At the grave, when the corpse is laid in the earth, the minister shall say,

Man that is born of a woman hath but a short time to live, and is full of misery. He cometh up, and is cut down like a flower ; he fleeth as it were a shadow, and never continueth in one stay.

In the midst of life we are in death : of whom may we seek for succor, but of thee, O Lord, who for our sins art justly displeased ?

Yet, O Lord God most holy, O Lord most mighty, O holy and most merciful Saviour, de-liver us not into the bitter pains of eternal death.

Thou knowest, Lord, the secrets of our hearts : shut not thy merciful ears to our pray-ers, but spare us, Lord most holy, O God most mighty, O holy and merciful Saviour, thou most worthy Judge eternal, suffer us not at our last hour for any pains of death to fall from thee.

Then shall be said,

I heard a voice from heaven saying unto me, Write; from henceforth blessed are the dead who die in the Lord: even so, saith the Spirit; for they rest from their labors.

Then shall the minister say,

Lord have mercy upon us.
Christ have mercy upon us.
Lord have mercy upon us.

Our Father who art in heaven, hallowed be thy name; thy kingdom come; thy will be

done on earth as it is in heaven: Give us this
day our daily bread, and forgive us our trespasses, as we forgive them that trespass against us;
and lead us not into temptation; but deliver us
from evil. *Amen.*

The Collect.

O merciful God, the Father of our Lord Jesus
Christ, who is the resurrection and the life; in
whom whosoever believeth shall live, though he
die: and whosoever liveth and believeth in him
shall not die eternally; We meekly beseech
thee, O Father, to raise us from the death of sin
unto the life of righteousness; that when we
shall depart this life we may rest in him; and
at the general resurrection on the last day may
be found acceptable in thy sight, and receive
that blessing which thy well beloved Son shall
then pronounce to all that love and fear thee,
saying, Come ye blessed of my Father, receive
the kingdom prepared for you from the beginning of the world.   Grant this, we beseech thee,
O merciful father, through Jesus Christ our Mediator and Redeemer. *Amen.*

The grace of our Lord Jesus Christ, and the
love of God, and the fellowship of the Holy
Ghost, be with us all evermore. *Amen.*

CHAPTER XII.

OF SUPPORT AND SUPPLIES.

SECTION I.

Of the Allowance to the Ministers and Preachers, and to their Wives, Widows, and Children.

1. The annual allowance of the married traveling, supernumerary, and superannuated preachers, shall be two hundred dollars, and their traveling expenses.

2. The annual allowance of the unmarried traveling, supernumerary, and superannuated preachers, shall be one hundred dollars, and their traveling expenses.

3. Each child of a traveling preacher shall be allowed sixteen dollars annually, to the age of seven years, and twenty-four dollars annually from the age of seven to fourteen years; and those preachers whose wives are dead shall be allowed for each child annually a sum sufficient to pay the board of such child or children during the above term of years: *Nevertheless*, this rule shall not apply to the children of preachers whose families are provided for by other means in their circuits respectively.

4. The annual allowance of the widows of traveling and superannuated preachers, shall be one hundred dollars.

5. The orphans of traveling, superannuated,

and worn-out preachers, shall be allowed by the Annual Convention the same sums respectively which are allowed to the children of living preachers. And on the death of a preacher leaving a child or children without so much of worldly goods as should be necessary to his, her, or their support, the Annual Convention of which he was a member shall raise, in such manner as may be deemed best, a yearly sum for the subsistence and education of such orphan child or children, until he, she, or they, shall have arrived at fourteen years of age. The amount of which yearly sum shall be fixed by a committee of the Convention at each session in advance.

6. It shall be the duty of a committee appointed by the Official Board, who shall be members of our Church, to make an estimate of the amount necessary to furnish fuel and table expenses for the family or families of preachers stationed with them, which estimate shall be subject to the action of the Official Board; and the Stewards shall provide, by such means as they may devise, to meet such expenses, in money or otherwise: *provided* the Stewards shall not appropriate the moneys collected for the regular quarterly allowance of the preachers to the payment of family expenses.

Let every class leader at the commencement of the year, ascertain how much each member of his class is able and willing to pay, *per week*, for the suppport of the preachers, and note the same in his class-book, and diligently see to it that the collections are made weekly, duly credited, and paid over to the Steward for the benefit of the preachers.

7. Let the Stewards circulate among our friends a subscription, payable quarterly, to supply the deficiency in the preacher's allowance; and if there be any surplus arising from the class collections and the quarterly subscriptions, it shall be appropriated for the support of missions, unless otherwise ordered by the official board.

SECTION II.

Of the Qualifications, Appointments, and Duties of the Stewards of Circuits and Stations.

Quest. 1. What are the qualifications necessary for Stewards?

Answ. Let them be men of solid piety, who both know and love the Methodist doctrine and discipline, and of good natural and acquired abilities to transact the temporal business.

Quest. 2. How are Stewards to be appointed?

Answ. By the Society at their annual meeting.

Quest. 3. What are the duties of Stewards?

Answ. To take an exact account of all the money or other provisions collected for the support of preachers in the circuit; to make an accurate return of every expenditure of money, whether to the preachers, the sick, or the poor; to seek the needy and distressed in order to re-

lieve and comfort them ; to inform the preachers
of any sick or disorderly persons; to tell the
preachers what they think wrong in them; to
attend the quarterly meetings of their circuit; to
give advice, if asked, in planning the circuit;
to attend committees for the application of money
to Churches; to give counsel in matters of arbitration; provide elements for the Lord's supper;
to write circular letters to the societies in the
circuit to be more liberal if need be ; as also to
let them know, when occasion requires, the state
of the temporal concerns at the last quarterly
meeting; to register the marriages and baptisms.

Quest. 4. What number of Stewards are necessary in each circuit?

Answ. Not less than than three, nor more than
nine, one of whom shall be the Recording Steward.

CHAPTER XIII.

Missions.

1. Each Annual Convention shall have the
charge of all missions within its bounds. It
shall have power to employ missionaries to labor within its bounds, who, with the concurrence of the president, shall be authorized to
establish new churches, where the interests of
the cause of God require.

2. Each class leader shall appoint a missionary collector for his class, who shall collect at

least a cent a week for each member of the class who is willing to contribute the same; and from any persons not members of our Church who are willing to contribute to our missionary fund.

3. A public missionary collection shall also be taken up at each appointment on every circuit.

4. All moneys collected for missionary purposes shall be taken to the Annual Convention, and applied according to its direction.

COURSE OF STUDY

For those who wish to join the Traveling Connection on probation

English Grammar, Arithmetic, Modern Geography, Free Methodist Discipline, Spelling and Composition.

FOR TRAVELING PREACHERS.

FIRST YEAR.

The Bible—Doctrines.

The Existence of God; the Attributes of God, namely, Unity, Spirituality, Eternity, Omnipotence, Ubiquity, Omniscience, Immutability, Wisdom, Truth, Justice, Mercy, Love, Goodness,

Holiness; the Trinity in Unity; the Deity of
Christ; the Humanity of Christ; the Union of
Deity and Humanity; Personality and Deity of
the Holy Ghost; Depravity; Atonement; Re-
pentance; Justification by Faith; Regeneration;
Adoption; the Witness of the Spirit; Growth in
Grace; Christian Perfection; Possibility of Final
Apostacy; Immortality of the Soul; Resurrec-
tion of the Body; General Judgment; Rewards
and Punishment.

Watson's Institutes, First Part; Wesley's
Plain Account of Christian Perfection; Cutter's
Anatomy and Physiology; Caldwell's Elocution.

Composition.

Essay or Sermon.
[Read Wesley's Sermons and Notes; The
Life of Wesley; Platt's Gift of Power; Way-
land's Political Economy.]

SECOND YEAR.

The Bible—Sacraments.

The Sacrament of Baptism—Its Nature, Design, Obligation, Subjects, and Mode; The Sacrament of the Lord's Supper—Its Nature, Design, and Obligation.

Watson's Institutes, Second Part to the 18th
Chapter; Peck's Central Idea; Wayland's Moral Science.

Composition.

Essay or Sermon.

[Read Bangs' History of Methodism; Johnston's Natural Philosophy.]

THIRD YEAR.

The Bible—History and Chronology.

Candidates to be prepared upon the leading events in the Old and New Testament; Reference Books; Horne's Introduction; and Robinson's Palestine.

Watson's Institutes, Second Part, beginning with the 18th Chapter; Paley's Natural Theology; Ruter's Church History; Whateley's Logic; Boyd's Rhetoric.

Composition.

Essay or Sermon.

[Read Fletcher's Works; Smith's Patriarchal Age; Wilson's Outlines of History.]

FOURTH YEAR.

Review of the whole course. Watson's Institutes, Third and Fourth Parts; Butler's Analogy; Hitchcock's Elementary Geology.

Composition.

Essay or Sermon.

[Read Smith's Hebrew People; Mosheim's Ecclesiastical History; Wayland's Intellectual Philosophy; History of the United States.

www.ingramcontent.com/pod-product-compliance
Lightning Source LLC
Chambersburg PA
CBHW020041040426
42331CB00030B/122